THE SOCIETY OF TO-MORROW

AN IMPORTANT TRANSLATION.

THE ENGLISH PEOPLE:

A STUDY OF ITS POLITICAL PSYCHOLOGY.

By Émile Boutmy, Membre de l'Institut, Author of "The English Constitution" and "Studies in Constitutional Law." Translated from the French by E. English. With an Introduction by J. E. C. Bodley, Author of "France."

Demy 8vo, cloth, 16s.

LONDON: T. FISHER UNWIN.

THE SOCIETY OF TO-MORROW · A FORECAST OF ITS POLITICAL AND ECONOMIC ORGANISATION

By G. [Gustave] DE MOLINARI

Correspondant de l'Institut, and Editor-in-Chief of "Le Journal des Economistes"

TRANSLATED BY P. H. LEE WARNER WITH A LETTER TO THE PUBLISHER FROM FRÉDÉRIC PASSY AND AN INTRODUCTION BY HODGSON PRATT

LONDON: T. FISHER UNWIN
PATERNOSTER SQUARE · MCMIV

Originally published in 1899.
Translated to English in 1904.

Large Print Edition published 2012 by Skyler J. Collins.
Visit: www.skylerjcollins.com

Cover image by StockFreeImages.com.

ISBN-13: 978-1479306329
ISBN-10: 1479306320

CONTENTS

	PAGE
INTRODUCTION BY HODGSON PRATT	ix
LETTER TO THE PUBLISHER FROM FRÉDÉRIC PASSY	xxviii
PREFACE—THE LAWS OF NATURE	xxx

PART I

THE STATE OF WAR

CHAP.		PAGE
I.	FORMATION OF PRIMITIVE COMMUNITIES AND THE CONDITIONS NECESSARY TO THEIR EXISTENCE	1
II.	COMPETITION BETWEEN PRIMITIVE COMMUNITIES AND ITS RESULTS	6
III.	COMPETITION BETWEEN STATES IN PROCESS OF CIVILISATION	10
IV.	DECLINE OF DESTRUCTIVE COMPETITION	13
V.	WHY THE STATE OF WAR CONTINUES WHEN IT NO LONGER FULFILS A PURPOSE	19
VI.	CONSEQUENCES OF THE PERPETUATION OF THE STATE OF WAR	29

Contents

PART II

THE STATE OF PEACE

CHAP.		PAGE
I.	THE COLLECTIVE GUARANTEE OF THE SECURITY OF NATIONS	38
II.	THE FREE CONSTITUTION OF NATIONALITY	47
III.	FREE CONSTITUTION OF GOVERNMENTS AND THEIR NATURAL FUNCTIONS	58
IV.	FREE CONSTITUTION OF GOVERNMENTS AND THEIR NATURAL FUNCTIONS (*continued*)	65
V.	FREE CONSTITUTION OF GOVERNMENTS AND THEIR NATURAL FUNCTIONS (*continued*)	75
VI.	SUBJECTION AND SOVEREIGNTY OF THE INDIVIDUAL	81
VII.	IMPOST AND CONTRIBUTION	87
VIII.	PRODUCTION OF ARTICLES OF NATURALLY INDIVIDUAL CONSUMPTION	96
IX.	EQUILIBRIUM OF PRODUCTION AND CONSUMPTION	102
X.	DISTRIBUTION OF PRODUCTS AND THE SHARE OF CAPITAL IN THE PROCEEDS OF PRODUCTION	114
XI.	DISTRIBUTION OF PRODUCTS AND THE SHARE OF LABOUR IN THE PROCEEDS OF PRODUCTION	124
XII.	THE PROBLEM OF POPULATION	133
XIII.	CONSUMPTION	144
XIV.	THE EXPANSION OF CIVILISATION	154
XV.	SUMMARY AND CONCLUSION	163

Contents

PART III

APPENDIX

		PAGE
NOTE A.	THE CZAR AND DISARMAMENT	175
,, B.	SYNDICATES RESTRICTING COMPETITION, OR "TRUSTS"	192
,, C.	EFFECTS OF INDUSTRIAL PROGRESS ON THE SPHERE OF PRODUCTION	196
,, D.	COSTS AND PROFITS OF STATE COLONISATION	198
,, E.	THE ECONOMIC AND SOCIALIST CONCEPTIONS OF THE SOCIETY OF THE FUTURE	204

Introduction

It is fortunate for the modern world that there is a considerable number of persons who have time, inclination, and ability to inquire how human communities may best secure a prosperous existence and ultimate salvation from disasters or even annihilation. It is fortunate that the necessity is so widely felt of making such inquiries, and that there is so great an accumulation of facts, and of arguments based thereon, as to enable thinkers to arrive at a complete knowledge of the dangers which menace society, and of the best way of dealing with them. We greatly need light from men who are capable of giving answers to such questions as the following: "What should be the definite aim of all human societies? Whither tend the communities and nations now in existence? What are their special dangers, and how can they best be averted? What should be the true ideals of every people, so that they may be kept clearly in view and realised?"

Such wise and thoughtful books as that of M. de Molinari, the well-known and most distinguished

Introduction

economist, should be carefully studied by all who care for the welfare of their fellow-men. He stimulates thought and consideration regarding these great problems, and produces masses of fact and argument, which enable his readers to think solidly and effectively.

Few can read his book without perceiving clearly how great are the problems which statesmen, philosophers, and philanthropists have to face. It is madness and treachery to trust to things " finding their level." Peoples, as well as individuals, must know to what point in the chart of humanity they should steer—where are the rocks and shoals, what is the best and shortest route. At all events in these days, more than ever before, there are moral, political, and social geographers, eager to point the true course and to awaken their fellows to the overwhelming importance of the inquiry.

There are, as we know, two great schools of social reformers, guides and teachers—the School of Individualists and the School of Organisers, if we may use the term : (1) Those who consider it sufficient to provide a fair field for liberty and free competition to all engaged in the " struggle for life " ; and (2) those who say that there is no such thing as " equality of opportunity " for the millions, and that, without most perfect organisation in the interests of those millions, the poor only grow poorer and the rich

Introduction

richer—misery for the many, luxury for the few.

Here is the great question which should occupy the minds of all who desire that the human world should not be a ghastly failure. Here we have before us the question presented under the title of "The Future of Society," to quote the title of M. de Molinari's book. It may be termed the question of realising that long-desired end, the greatest happiness of the greatest number. To bring this great problem vividly before the reader, we cannot do better than make a quotation from an author who puts the whole case somewhat as follows : " Half a century ago, I conceived the possibility of coming to an understanding between the two Schools, and I addressed them as follows : ' What is the Ideal alike common to Socialists and Economists? It is surely this: the realisation of a state of society in which the production of all good and necessary things, advantages or welfare necessary to maintain and embellish life, shall be the most abundant possible, and wherein the distribution of these things amongst those who produce them shall be the most equitable possible —in a word, Abundance and Justice. But we proceed to this end by different routes—you by an obscure path which you call the organisation of labour ; we, the economists, by the broad and well-known highway of Liberty. Why do you refuse the latter ? "Because," say you, "it is

Introduction

the rule of the privileged classes interested in maintaining the present policy of war and aggression. Then, and then only, will be set free the resources and the energies of the industrial populations, who, being released from the present burdens, will all have a fair share of the results of their labour. In effect, he says, "carry out this great change, and there will be no need for such fancied remedies as are promised by Socialism."

It is, indeed, of vital importance that the people of every country in Europe should seek a remedy for the enormous evils from which they suffer,—one which shall be complete and far-reaching. A great service, therefore, is rendered, as a first step in the reform needed, when an authoritative and trusted teacher of economic science denounces the rule of the militarist and governing classes. He does so because he knows it is hopeless to attempt the abolition of social misery and anarchy until the peoples are relieved from their present intolerable burdens.

Hear what this careful master of statistics says: "Two-thirds of the European budgets consist of charges for war and debts. The premium paid for ensuring 'security' exceeds the risk." "The total expenditure, direct and indirect, absorbs half the wealth produced by the working classes." The governments must therefore be deprived of their unlimited power over the life and fortune

Introduction

of the citizens, and that power will continue so long as the existing state of war or armed peace continues. The States of Europe have accumulated more than 130 milliards of debt, or 5,900,000,000 in pounds sterling. Yet, while these charges continually rise, industrial productivity tends to fall off.

The object of the governing class has been to secure profit from fresh conquests, in order that the advantages may be divided between civil and military officers; while the loss involved has fallen in an increasing degree upon industry, and the flower of the race has been absorbed for purposes of war. "Hence," says our author, "the most urgent reform of the present time is to put an end to this latent state of conflict," and he asserts that the remedy is to be found in a "collective insurance" against war. There should be a joint insurance to provide for the collective protection of States, instead of the present "isolated insurance." He is further of opinion that the ruinous effects of war upon neutral and non-belligerent States gives them a right to intervene, whenever other States propose to engage in conflict. In fact, he proposes the substitution of "collective justice" for the present claim of each Government to be a judge of its own rights. M. de Molinari, therefore, suggests that Europe should constitute an association strong enough to oblige any single nation to submit its disputes to an arbitral court; and that this should be supple-

Introduction

mented by troops sufficient to enforce the verdict of the tribunal. By such provisions individual governments would no longer claim that they have the duty of providing insurance against war, and all excuse for unlimited disposal of the lives and property of their peoples would cease. With the great political change thus inaugurated would come an immense increase in individual liberty, "individual sovereignty" being the required basis of the political institutions of the future; so that the resources of a nation would no longer be at the mercy of a class, and the individual would become his own master.

The "individualist ideal" is that under which all the citizens would be associated, not only for common security, but for all public ends connected with municipal life. Then State taxation would be greatly reduced, local services being provided for by rates. This would lead to a great extension of productive enterprise, at present hampered and impeded, and there would be a great impetus given to individual activity through increased freedom. M. de Molinari has a firm faith in the great results of unlimited "competition" which would tend to reduce prices to the level of the cost of production; and he says that, with growing enterprise, new markets will be found, and so a demand for skilled labour increase; while the growth of machinery will diminish existing inequalities in remuneration.

Introduction

The price of the product being diminished by machinery, new markets will grow up and, with them, more demand for skilled labour. This means an increase of consumption and increased means of providing for it.

We must leave students of economics to consider M. de Molinari's statement of the comparative advantages of a condition of things where competition shall have freer play and where the laws shall interfere as little as possible with the conditions under which industry is at present conducted (at least in some countries). He compares the results which will thus be obtained with the results of socialistic organisation—of course to the disadvantage of the latter.

His hope for the future is based not on any fundamental change in the organisation of industry, but on the greater control exercised over governments by the populations—in a word, on the growth of individual liberty.

Under the action of great " natural laws" which regulate the growth of society, civilisation has grown up, and M. de Molinari asks whether the progress accomplished has not diminished the sum of human suffering ; but this question he leaves undecided. " Increased happiness for man may," he says, " be the result of progress but not the object. That object is the increase of the power of the human race, in view of a destiny which is unknown to us."

Introduction

These are the final words of his book; and some philosophers may be content with that conclusion. It will not, however, satisfy the daily growing number of those who are in consternation at the existing condition of society, and who find their own lives made unhappy by the present order of things; one in which millions of men and women in the most "civilised" communities, lead an existence which makes them wish they had never been born, which makes the lot of the beast of the field seem enviable—lives, in which all that most distinguishes man from the animal is almost unattainable—lives from which all noble hopes and purposes, all glorious and divine enjoyments are utterly shut out.

This is truly the age of great cities; but what an amount of chaotic misery that implies! In those great cities of London, or Glasgow, or Liverpool, or Birmingham, how many thousands of parents rise every morning asking themselves how their sons and daughters are to live—it is a mere lottery whether it shall be success or failure. Their education is, in a vast number of cases, ill adapted to their respective needs; and their avocations will therefore be decided by mere chance. A lad will become a carpenter, a blacksmith, a shop assistant or a clerk, a soldier or a sailor by haphazard. "The square pegs are put into round holes, and the round into square." And in a vast number of cases nothing but failure

Introduction

is the result. To many it must seem to be a better lot for a man to be born in a Hindoo or Burmese village than in a London street. At all events, in the former a child's future trade or profession is settled beforehand by his caste or class, and he is prepared for it designedly from his first years.

In view of the justifiable dismay which many of us feel, I venture to think that M. de Molinari should not have dismissed the proposals of the Socialist schools with such scant reference as being simply the result of "ignorance," and the "negation of the natural laws which govern mankind." It seems to me that any attempt to frame a "Future of Society" should at least include an inquiry into the economic theory called "Collectivism."

What indeed is the Socialist demand, as the fundamental condition of a human society which professes to be governed by a desire for the moral welfare of all its members—for which right economic conditions are indispensable? The great revolution demanded is that of the substitution of Collectivism for Individualism. If the latter has quite failed to provide for the well-being of the great majority of the population in civilised countries, the demand for the former should be heard.

The aim of every rightly constituted human society is the greatest possible happiness of the greatest possible number. But under the exist-

Introduction

ing haphazard and non-organised conditions, there is none of that equality of opportunity which is essential if individual liberty is to suffice for the attainment of the end in view. At present all is confusion and waste of means, because there is no guarantee that each man shall do the work for which he is best fitted, and be properly trained for it. Unregulated competition is at present the only resource for the members of a community ignorant of the conditions which are essential to a right use of capital and labour. The result is that while some members of the community are idle, others are the slaves of excessive toil, and a third group are doing work for which they are unfitted. This is well pointed out by Mr. J. A. Hobson in his admirable work on " The Social Problem." He reminds us of the results of this want of intelligent adaptation of means to the end in England. Three-fourths of our town population live under unhealthy and almost intolerable conditions, and, as he says, no increase of the total amount of material wealth can compensate for such deterioration of work and life as is going on among millions of men and women. In view of such facts is it not justifiable to assert that there is no hope without organisation on the part of the community ? Adoption of methods capable of providing a decent existence, on the doctrine of " All for each, and each for all," is an imperative requirement.

Introduction

This is what the Socialist asserts, and he has a right to say to the orthodox economist, What plan have you for remedying the tremendous evils of modern society, beyond the mere affirmation of certain axioms? There is no sufficient remedy in individual liberty. A large proportion of the community are handicapped by general chaos and confusion, and are ignorant of everything needed to give certainty of remunerative labour—it is a blind struggle of rival workers and distributors.

Yet this is the competition which is to rescue vast populations from their present misery and hopelessness!

The error of orthodox economists, it seems to me, has been to consider only how the sum total of national wealth may be increased, while disregarding the question of its distribution. Yet it should be possible to provide, in a large degree, for every member of the community to do that particular work which best enables him to live up to a decent standard of existence. When we find a state of things exist in which needlewomen earn only eighteen pence a day for more than twelve hours' labour, the whole community suffers as well as the worker, both morally and physically. It is not true civilisation; it is a barbarism which disgraces every member of the community, especially those who have the knowledge and opportunity for bringing about a change. Those who grow rich and powerful out of such an industrial *régime*

Introduction

participate in robbery, and cannot justify their position in the world.

The realisation of the ideals of the Socialist reformers means, of course, an entire transformation of existing social conditions, especially in a country such as England. Here the monopoly of the land by hereditary owners involves loss to the whole community. These owners can waste it on private enjoyment, and claim an exclusive right to the enormous national weath lying under the surface, for which their predecessors paid not one farthing. There can be no right conditions of existence so long as such a monopoly exists, and there can be no means of betterment for those who produce the national wealth by their daily labour, so long as this authorised injustice prevails. In the meantime the population becomes wholly urban, unable to live on the land.

. . . . .

It should be noted, however, that there has appeared during the last half-century a voluntary organisation known by the name of "Co-operation.' It has accomplished remarkable results in diminishing the misery of a great number of hand-workers, and in laying the foundation of a new system of production, distribution, and exchange, while giving new hope of social and economic amelioration. This remarkable work has been carried out by the more enlightened and self-reliant members of the proletariat, aided, here and there, by a few

Introduction

servants of humanity such as Robert Owen, Leclaire, Godin, E. Vansittart Neale, Charles Robert, and Schultze Delitsch.

In Great Britain there are two million members of these societies, and their organisation is on a vast scale, carried out with great administrative ability, and the best social and moral aims are not overlooked. It appears to me that no student of "the Future of Society" should neglect to appraise the true value and possibilities of such an organisation. The great purpose to be kept in view is the realisation, in every community, of the highest kind of existence possible for all its members; and that object has never been lost sight of by the Central Union of Co-operators. It does credit to the representatives of Labour in several European countries, that this movement has made great progress. It is capable of much further development, alike in spheres of production and trade. It is the best school of training for those who will, in the future, be charged with the duty of conducting municipal life on an increasing scale. It will also train men for the realisation of the changes which the Socialists entertain.

Indeed, Co-operation is in some degree an adoption of socialistic principles, in so far as individual association can succeed, and in the absence of the direct agency of the State. Co-operation, as in the case of Socialism, has in view a new social order,

Introduction

Its greatest object is to accomplish the equitable distribution of the proceeds of labour amongst all who have contributed to its result. In co-operation the labourers provide the capital or hire it, instead of being themselves hired by capital, as its veteran prophet, G. J. Holyoake, has declared in hundreds of speeches. The material results of a half-century of these societies can be shown in figures, though not the moral results, which are of no small value. Looking at the last Annual Report of the Central Co-operative Board, we find that the number of members (in 1671 societies) is considerably upwards of two millions, and that they hold shares of the value of nearly ninety-six millions sterling; the sales for the year were eighty-five and a half millions, yielding profits of nine and a half millions. These represented what is called the "Distributive" part of the organisation; while the Productive and Farming Societies embraced 34,875 members, with a capital of £881,568, the sales amounting to upwards of three millions. The productive outturn of individual societies and of the wholesale societies of England and Scotland combined is estimated at seven millions and a half.

"The co-operative conception of life," says the organ of the movement, the *Co-operative News*, "embraces the absence of all preventable waste through needless competition in social and political strife; when realised wholly, there would be no idle shopkeepers, no strikes and lockouts. Co-

Introduction

operation, when applied to national life, would not stop short at distribution, production and carriage, but would apply itself to planning or replanning cities, to education, to houses. The co-operative conception of life does not admit of any industrial hands remaining idle or of any capable minds lying fallow." It was because the Rochdale pioneers set out with the avowed aim of "making the world better than they found it," that their successors, labouring men and artisans, have done a work unsurpassed of its kind because spontaneous and without any reliance upon outside help or Government interference. Necessarily there are limits to such individual organisation; and this is the justification of the desire to revolutionise the whole industry of a nation as proposed by the Socialists.

. . . . .

The above reference to the moral elements at work in co-operation and to their frank recognition by its foremost leaders brings us to the greatest question of all : How far will any proposed change of economic conditions secure the truest welfare of men ?—in other words, How far can man's progress in all that is highest and best be secured ? However ingeniously devised new schemes of social and industrial improvement may be, whatever provision may be made for individual liberty, the rule of the Moral Law is the one condition of all true and sound progress. The Economic

Introduction

"laws," referred to by M. de Molinari, however fully recognised and followed by action, will not secure society from catastrophes, even when an enlightened self-interest may lead to the abolition of war. It will not wholly diminish strife and violence, either within or without, unless the moral law is generally observed. The "old Adam" will frequently reappear without it; and it is a profound error to ignore the fact.

The hope that the realisation of Socialism may rescue human communities from the tremendous evils which now oppress them is based on the fact that its aim is profoundly ethical, if not religious. It recognises the essential need of justice in all the departments of human life. It is because right conditions of life are necessary for the formation of human *character* that they are so important; and without character there is no guarantee of right *conduct*; and conduct is the basis of all well-being in society. The aim of socialism may therefore fairly be said to be the moral welfare of society. And under what other system of society, under what so-called laws is it proposed to secure right economic conditions? What other and better methods are suggested by those who profess to be economists?

Mr. Frederic Harrison has said that the real cause of all industrial evils is to be found in the want of a higher moral spirit in those engaged in industry. "The kingdom of God," it has been said, "is on

Introduction

the earth, and is concerned with all departments of human life." Altruism, not egoism, is the highest good of the individual, and its realisation is to be found in making the good of all the end of our individual action. "All for each, and each for all"—as the Co-operators have always said. No nobler watchword could have been adopted.

The highest self-interest, whether for individuals or communities, is fidelity to moral principle. To realise one's own highest good we must live for the good of others; and Christianity makes all things subservient to Brotherhood. "The toughest economic, social, and political questions must be solved by ethics—which teach that solidarity rooted in fraternity must be the basis of social relations."[1]

M. de Molinari and other economists treat their science as a study of men's actions in the business of life, and infer that men will at all times act in the same way and from the same motives. But is this true? Are there not elements at work in modern communities which were absent at previous periods? There exists now a widespread feeling of moral solidarity and fraternity which was once unknown, and which exercises an increasing influence on laws, on conduct, and on institutions. It is, therefore, a profound error to separate the study of economics from that of ethical, social, political, and religious science.

[1] "The Foundations of Society," by John Wilson Harper.

Introduction

There are immense possibilities within reach of that future "new moral world" which will be based on the universal recognition of Fraternity. Every man that hath that hope in him will become the nobler, and will work the harder for its realisation. There will be an ever-increasing approach to a perfect state of society, "when man shall be liker man through all the cycles of the Golden Year."

HODGSON PRATT.

LE PECQ (SEINE ET OISE), FRANCE.

Prefatory Letter

TO MR. FISHER UNWIN

You are about to publish an English version of my friend M. de Molinari's book, "La Société Future," and you do me the honour to request a few lines of introduction from my pen. To write adequately of such a book would require time that my age and obligations do not, unfortunately, permit me to give. Since, however, the opportunity does occur, I should be most unwilling to let the book appear without at least testifying my esteem and admiration for the character and talent of the man who is to-day, unless I am mistaken, the doyen of our economists—I should say of our liberal economists — of the men with whom, though, alas! few in number, I have been happy to stand side by side during more than half a century.

Their principles were proclaimed and defended in England through the mouths of Adam Smith, Fox, Cobden, Gladstone, and Bright. In France they were championed by Quesnay, Turgot, Say, Michel Chevalier, Laboulaye, and Bastiat. And my belief grows yearly stronger that, but for these principles, the societies of the present would

Prefatory Letter

be without wealth, peace, material greatness, or moral dignity.

Monsieur de Molinari has maintained these principles from his youth, from the day when—at the epoch of our Revolution of 1848—he first upheld them at the Soirées de la Rue St. Lazare. His "Conversations Familières sur la Commerce des Grains" gave them a new and attractive shape. He has defended his convictions both in his regular courses of lectures and also in those other lectures by means of which he has spread his principles even within the borders of Russia. Month by month the important Review of which he is editor-in-chief repeats them in a fresh guise; and annually, so to speak, a further book, as distinguished for clearness of grasp as for admirable literary style, goes out to testify to the constancy of his convictions no less than to the unimpaired vigour of his mental outlook and the virile serenity of his green old age.

The book which you are about to introduce to the English public is, in some sort, a summing-up of his long studies of the past, his clear-sighted observations upon the present, and his shrewd predictions for the future. You, Sir, do well when you endeavour to obtain for it that additional publicity which it deserves; and I count myself fortunate that you have permitted me to contribute, in however small a degree, to so admirable an end.

FRÉDÉRIC PASSY.

Preface

THE LAWS OF NATURE

"IF," wrote Condorcet, "there is a science which forecasts, guides, and promotes the advance of the human race, it must be based on the records of past progress."[1] But we must go back still further. We must return to the first causes of that progress which the human race has realised since its appearance upon earth, and of the progress that it is still destined to realise. We must have an understanding of man, the laws which determine and govern his activities, the nature and circumstances of the environment in which he has been placed for the fulfilment of a purpose still hidden from his eyes.

I. THE MOTIVE OF HUMAN ACTIVITY.

Man is an organism composed of vital, physical, intellectual, and moral forces. This matter and these forces, which form the individual and the

[1] Condorcet, "Esquisse d'un Tableau Historique des Progrès de l'Esprit Humain," p. 17.

The Motive of Human Activity

species, can only be preserved and developed by the assimilation, or, to use the economic term, the consumption of materials and forces of like nature. Failing this consumption, their vitality wastes and is finally extinguished. But waste and extinction of vitality cause pain and suffering, and it is the stimulus of pain and suffering which impels man to acquire the materials necessary for the development and preservation of his life. All these materials are present in his environment, air, &c.; and nature gives him a small number free of cost. But with the exception of this minority they must be discovered, acquired, and adapted to the purposes of consumption. Man must be a *producer*.

Man is also subject to a further necessity, one which is again inherent in his environment. He must defend both life and the means of its support from the attacks of numerous spoilers and agents of destruction. The risks to which he is exposed under this head entail more pain and more endurance.

It is to meet this twofold need—sustenance and self-defence—that man labours, labours to produce the necessaries of consumption and to destroy the agents or elements that menace his security. Labour therefore implies waste of vital force, and this more endurance and more pain. Humanity is, however, compensated by the pleasure and enjoyment which it derives from consuming the

Preface

materials that support life, and from providing the services that safeguard it. But always, whether there be question of nourishment or self-defence, the pleasure of these actions is bought with a pain. It is an exchange, and, like every other exchange, it may result in a profit or loss. It is profitable when the sum of vitality, acquired or preserved, exceeds the amount of vital force expended in the task. The product may be concrete or one of service, but it is always subject to the costs of production which are inseparable from every expenditure of force.

Excess of expenditure over receipts means, on the other hand, loss, so that man is only stimulated to work when he expects that his receipts will exceed his expenses, that the pleasure will outweigh the pain. The degree of the stimulus naturally varies with the sums involved and the rate of expected profit; the prime motive of human activity, no less than that of all other creatures, is, therefore, the hope of profit. This motive, or motor-power, has been called *interest*.[1]

---

[1] The economist must not confound interest with selfishness, still less with the satisfaction of such needs as are purely material. It signifies rather the sum of the requirements of human nature, material as well as moral. A man does not impose upon himself the sufferings which are inseparable from effort, nor abstain from enjoying the fruits of his toil, for the sole purpose of satisfying selfish wants, whether present or future. Altruistic intention is a frequent and often the more powerful factor in determining labours or abstentions. Altruism includes the love of family and the

Law of the Economy of Power

II. THE NATURAL LAW OF THE ECONOMY OF POWER, OR THE LAW OF LEAST EXPENDITURE.

From the motive of which we have spoken, the roots of which lie deep in human nature and the conditions of human existence, we derive a first natural law, the *Law of Economy in Production*, or the *Law of Least Expenditure*. Under the spur of interest, man first satisfies his most pressing needs, those that appeal with the greatest urgency, or penalise deficient supply with the greatest amount of suffering. It is only after this that he endeavours to decrease expenditure by selecting the more remunerative spheres of activity, and by setting himself to perfect processes, or invent tools, which enable him to enhance the profits of production. By increasing

race, of truth and justice; and its scope is only limited by that of the moral sentiment. Under its spur men have died for each other, a cause, even a cherished idea. There is no real warrant for the opposition between interest and duty, a contradiction that has been too often reiterated. Duty is no more than the obligation to act in conformity with justice, the criterion of which is the general and permanent interest of the species. The sense of justice—in other words the moral sense—naturally predisposes us to conform action to duty. This sense is, no doubt, distributed most unequally. Certain individuals find that obedience to its dictates yields a joy which outweighs any pain, and such men pursue duty at all costs and in face of every obstacle; others are less conscious of the stimulus. A sense of obligation is often disobeyed, but every lapse is followed by that feeling of pain which is called remorse. Finally, there are many persons whose moral sense, the sense of justice, is quite rudimentary;

Preface

the margin of gain, enlarging the excess of material acquired or saved over the outlay of vital force, he also insures the preponderance of compensatory pleasure over the discomfort, which is inseparable from effort.

The individual whose income exceeds expenditure, who possesses a profit, may sink it in the purchase of immediate enjoyment, or collect it as capital to be employed in a further increase of his productive capacity. He may, also, simply hoard it against future need. It, then, serves the purpose of a twofold reserve, drafts upon which may obviate privations, or furnish the means of repelling such chances as may, hereafter, menace vitality. When individuals of the same, or of alien races, join issue as to who shall obtain the materials of subsistence, the victor is he who has

they commit every kind of injustice or immorality to satisfy their passions or vices, and are a menace to society and the race. Mere self-defence compels society to supplement such enfeebled sense of the obligations. It therefore imposes penalties, regulating their incidence in such a way that the amount of pleasure obtained by committing an injustice is more than neutralised by the punishment which follows.

Society's first duty is, therefore, to foster the sense of justice—the moral sense. And it is equally imperative to define the distinction between just and unjust, moral and immoral, since the hurt or benefit of society and the species is bound up with the opposition between these two ideas. The interests of the individual and the species are, in their regard, identical. (See the present author's "La Morale Economique," book i.—The Relation of Morality to Political Economy; see also his "Religion," chapter xii.—Religion and Science.)

The Law of Competition

devoted most profits to remunerative ends, to measures best fitted to conserve, or augment, his vital force.

III. The Natural Law of Competition for a Subsistence.

1. *Animal Competition.*—A struggle to acquire the means of living has been called competition for a subsistence. It invariably appears so soon as the natural supply of material ceases to suffice for the demands of every member of the community, the weak and strong alike. Early man, as yet uninstructed in artificial production, depended solely upon the provision of nature, and the consequences of a deficit were soon felt in a society living on the products of hunting and the natural fruits of the earth. The more effective members, the fleet hunter and skilled forager, excelled and lived; the feeble and less fitted for these tasks languished and passed away. Hence the original struggle, first manifestation of a principle which rules all created things, and which we have named Animal Competition.

2. *Destructive Competition, or the State of War.*—A progressive restriction in the natural sources of supply soon compelled even the most effective individual to pay a higher price for his accustomed share, and increased cost entailed increased suffering. With the amount of labour and effort, required for the purchase of a livelihood, in-

Preface

creasing in inverse ratio to the shrinkage of supply, palliative measures became inevitable. Two alternatives presented themselves—to restrict competition, or to multiply the sources of subsistence.

Now the sum of knowledge required for artificial production of the material necessaries of life is such that the highest intelligence fails unless accompanied by long experience. This is so true that, to this present day, it is beyond the capabilities of many backward tribes. Very simple, on the contrary, is the alternative as viewed by a strong man. Strength knows its own value as against a weak competitor. When, more, we see how incapable is the rest of brute creation to grasp this elementary calculation, we may find the first glimmering of man's superiority in his early appreciation of its truth.

The enterprise did, without doubt, involve a certain amount of labour and a certain risk. But victory in the struggles of unequals—and nowhere is there greater inequality than between members of the human race—does not always entail profound exertion, or the taking of dangerous risks. In any case, the strong soon learned that it was more profitable to prey upon the weak than to continue the previous system of sharing an inadequate food supply. Where it was customary to devour the actual body of the defeated, the new system was by so much the

The Law of Competition

more productive. In other words, the effort or suffering involved in destroying an inferior was held preferable to the alternative of dwelling in amity but eating insufficiently. The invariable choice of this alternative measures the expectation of profit which it offered. Where cannibalism intervened as an accident, the person of every victim was at once a meal gained and a meal—very many meals—saved.

This second form of destructive competition is the pure State of War. First originating in man's struggle for mastery over the beasts, the issue became one as between man and man. A State of War was, thenceforward, inseparable from human existence. As the prime motive of the construction of a vast armoury of destructive agencies, it directly assured the triumph of humanity over the beasts, though nature had often endowed them far more efficiently. Indirectly, it determined those industrial discoveries which have enabled man to multiply and artificially supplement nature's provision of the material bases of existence, instead of bowing his head with the beasts when spontaneous production lags in the race with his demands. Thus it came to pass that the strong no longer found it profitable to massacre, despoil, or yet devour his victims. Instead, obligations are imposed, and the victim survives as a serf or slave. Political States are formed and com-

Preface

petition in the form of war is waged between communities, possessing territory and subject peoples, against the hordes, still in a state of savagery and dependent upon the chase or pillage. The communities afterwards compete among themselves, seeking in territorial expansion either an extended area of supply or an increased holding in slaves, serfs, or subjects. Self-aggrandizement and self-protection are practically the sole ends of modern warfare.[1]

Progress, under the direct or indirect impulse of this second form of competition has engendered a third form—*Productive* or *Industrial* competition. A brief survey of its history shows us that a continual menace of destruction, or at least of dispossession, compelled the communities which founded, and owned, political States, to apply themselves to the improvement of their instruments, and the consolidation of the material bases of their power. These instruments, and this fabric, may be divided into two categories. Their first constituent is a destructive apparatus, an army; their second is a productive apparatus, capable of assuring subsistence to the proprietary community within the State, and also to its dependents. It must, in addition, furnish those advances which are necessary, first for the erection, and subsequently

[1] See the author's "Les Notions Fondamentales de l'Economie Politique," Introduction, page 5.

The Law of Competition

for the maintenance in working order, of the destructive apparatus. Under pressure of the State of War—and the more so as that pressure grew and increased—State-owning communities were impelled not merely to improve the art and engines of warfare, but also to promote the productive capacities of industries whose function was not merely to provide sustenance, but, through the support of the defensive establishment, to become the final foundation of their powers of political aggrandizement. Now expansion in the productive capacity of any industry depends upon two conditions—*Security*, and *Liberty*.

Without some assured title to the fruits of his progress, a producer has no motive for undertaking such costly labours as the discovery of new processes, or the invention of tools and machines, which will increase his output. It is further essential that a manufacturer should be free to devote himself to that particular industry to which his abilities are best fitted, and to offer his wares in those markets which yield the highest returns. The highest place in the hierarchy of the nations has gone to that State which secured the fullest liberty, and the greatest security, to its industrial population. The dominion of such a State increases with its strength, and the security and liberty which it guarantees initiated and developed the third form of competition—

Preface

Productive or *Industrial* competition. This form displaces the State of War as naturally as that replaced its predecessor in the series.

3. *Productive or Industrial Competition.*—Competition in the field of production, as in all others, benefits the species by affirming that: "*The race is to the fleet, the battle to the strong.*" But if the rivalries of war and of peace lead to one goal, it is by very different roads.

The means by which competition of the destructive, or warlike, kind proceeds, are direct. Two starveling tribes come to blows over a patch of vegetation or a tract of hunting ground, and the stronger—driving off, if it does not actually destroy, the weaker—seizes the means of subsistence which were the cause of their struggle. At the later stage, when mankind has learned artificial production of the material needs of life, the communities of strong men, which founded the commercial enterprises called States, fight for the possession of a territory and the subjection of its inhabitants. They, like their predecessors, seek the means of subsistence, and they hope to obtain them by appropriating the entire nett profit earned by the labour of their slaves, their serfs, or their subjects. They may annex this in the guise of forced labour, or under the name of taxes, and they may style their conduct political competition, but it differs in no single particular from the actions of a

The Law of Competition

hunting or of a marauding tribe. Both move along the straight road of direct competitive destruction, and both actions are of the class of destructive or warlike competition.

Very different are the processes of industrial competition, although they too issue in the survival of the strongest, of the fittest. The most powerful rival still takes the first place, but it no longer rests with the victor to proclaim, or to assess, his own victory. This function has passed to a third party—to those who consume the products or services which the competitors offer. The consumer always buys in the cheapest market. When he has once ascertained the precise nature of the wares competing for his custom, his own merchandise—and this may be actual produce, service, or the monetary equivalent of either—invariably selects that market in which it can command the highest return. When two markets are equal in this respect, the balance of trade inclines to that in which the purchaser's needs, or demands, are supplied with goods of the better quality.

The cheapest seller—all else being equal—commands the market, and the cheapest seller is the most powerful or effective producer. Productive or industrial competition, therefore, acts upon the producer by stimulating his powers and capacities of production. The less effective producer—whether of merchandise or services—

Preface

is penalised by failing to sell; he cannot, that is, obtain those other services and goods which he himself needs, and upon which his very existence depends. To increase their powers or capacities of production, producers apply the principle known as the Division of Labour. They also seek to invent, and make practical use of, processes, tools, and machines, by the use of which an identical expenditure of labour and suffering are enabled to return products, or services, in a constantly increasing ratio.

Productive competition is supported by the Law of the Economy of Power, and these two co-operate in furthering the advance of productive capacity. But while acting as a propeller, this same rivalry fulfils a second, and no less useful, function. As the pivot of a balance, it supports the scales that maintain equilibrium between supply and demand, between outlay and return, at the level of the price required to induce the creation of products or services. The motor-force, of our first view, now appears as a " governor," and its supporter in this regard is a new law—*the Law of Value.*

IV. THE NATURAL LAW OF VALUE.

Value is a power whose source resides in man himself. Its seat is the sum of those forces, vital, physical, and moral, with which man is endowed,

The Law of Value

and which he applies to the purposes of production or destruction. Applied to destruction, it constitutes military or war value, and while war was the sole sanction of security in the world this (aspect of) value was of most use to the species, and thus the most esteemed.[1] It does not, however, appear in the guise of an agency which regulates competition, until viewed from the standpoint of production.

Production acts through labour, and labour is an outlay of vital force, consequently of suffering. Also, the motive of this outlay is the expectation of profit. Profit is thus seen as a product of labour, which enables a man to purchase enjoyment, or to obviate a sum of suffering which is greater than the similar factor in his original outlay. Vital power expended in this manner is not lost, but re-embodied. It reappears, plus profit earned, in the product, and it constitutes the value of that product.

An isolated man consumes this value so soon as he has produced it. But to-day is the day of division of labour and of exchange—systems

[1] It need scarcely be added that destruction in the interests of security is a necessary factor in production. The ability to destroy constitutes military value. Whether manifested in clearing a territory of the wild beasts which infested it, or as a guarantee against the incursions of predatory tribes, it roots itself in the soil, and forms, so to speak, the first grounds for attaching value to that soil. (See the author's "Les Notions Fondamentales d'Economie Politique," chapter iv.—The Produce of the Earth.)

Preface

under which the producer offers commodities, in which value has been invested, for other commodities which he does not possess, or for that which will enable him to obtain those commodities—for money.

The ultimate motive of all exchange is identical, being the hope of obtaining a greater amount of vital power than was expended in producing the commodity offered by the seller. In economical language, it is the hope of recovering the costs of production plus a profit. The product offered by the seller must also furnish the consumer, the purchaser, with sufficient vital power—certainly with a sufficient restorative of his vitality, to induce him to purchase it with an equivalent sufficient to replace the vital power expended in production plus a profit. The degree of this profit varies with the relative value of the products in question. The producer seeks to raise it to the highest possible point, and the purchaser struggles to limit it to a minimum. The rate of profit is, however, determined by the point at which the comparative intensity of the needs, or desires, of the two parties to a bargain meet—the intensity of the seller's desire to sell and the intensity of the purchaser's desire to buy. These measures of desire translate themselves into terms of exchange as the quantity of his product, which either party offers—the amount of wares offered by the seller, and the amount of money

The Law of Value

offered by the purchaser. At this point we may conceive several variations in the position of seller and buyer.

One producer may meet one consumer.

One consumer may be met by several producers, or the position may be exactly reversed.

There may be sufficient consumers and sufficient producers to erect real competition on either side.

In every one of these hypothetical markets, prices, or the rate of exchange, will be determined by the comparative urgency of opposing desires. We shall, at the present moment, confine our attention to the third alternative. Then, if there are several sellers, and each carries a more or less full stock, the fear of being undersold by a rival will compel the merchants to successively increase the amounts which they offer at a given price. But the purchasers, having no fear of a failure in supply, will continually reduce the price which they are willing to pay. Prices will fall since there is no approximation of demand to supply. In a seller's market, where the sum of the desire to purchase outruns that of the desire to sell—of supply, a buyer's refusal to increase his bids may result in his failure to complete a purchase, and the tendency of price is upwards.

It is most essential to note that market prices do not solely follow the quantities offered, but develop according to a geometrical progression.

Preface

A short supply not only reduces market offers, but it also increases the effectiveness of demand; a glut in supply produces the opposite result, since the urgency of the seller increases while demand slackens. In one case the value of the product offered rises to a point which yields more than the required profit, over and above the actual costs of production; in the other, prices fall until profits may vanish and an actual loss set in.[1] It is now easy to understand the regulative action of competition. It is continually tending to "fix" exchange-value—in other words, to maintain prices at a point which is equal to the cost of production plus the amount of profit necessary to induce the producer to create the product, or service, which he seeks to sell. Adam Smith characteristically termed this the natural price. Over-supply and over-production cause a fall in the price-current, and as this fall results from an impulse which develops according to a geometrical progression, it very soon drops below the natural price. As soon as this point is reached production naturally tends to diminish, and the consequent gradual rise in the price-current frequently repasses the natural price and erects a surplus profit. But the movements of capital and labour invariably follow profits. As soon as a particular industry

[1] See the author's "Cours d'Economie Politique," Third Lesson—Value and Price.

The Law of Value

promises to return more than the normal rate of profit, capital and labour flow in; production is forced up by leaps and bounds, and the markets are once more filled to repletion. The socialistic cry for regulation, whether by the State or any other artificial authority, is therefore entirely absurd. Regulation is essential, but the two natural laws of Production and Value have long since joined to secure it. We need only refrain from throwing obstacles in the way of their regulative operation; or, if an artificial obstruction opposes that action, to guarantee their freedom in removing the obstruction, according to their own methods. Their action must be secured, but it is to be secured only by refraining from all interference.

Such is the motive, and such the laws, which govern human activity. The motive is Interest, and the laws are those of Least Expenditure, or Economy of Power, of Competition in its several forms, and of Value. Under the spur of this motive, and guided by these laws, man has achieved that progress which has raised him from the level of the brutes to civilisation, and has advanced through the State of War to the State of Peace.

As long as the State of War was an integral condition of existence, and of progress, this motive, and these laws, worked for the adaptation of political and social economics to that state.

Preface

When civilisation became the guarantee of security, and the State of War yielded to the State of Peace, the motive and the laws remained, but they worked to another end. And, from the point at which to-day stands on the long highroad of evolution, we may already look forward and prophecy concerning the political and economical organisation of the Society of To-morrow. Earlier volumes from my pen have foreshadowed that future. The arbitrary conceptions of the Socialist will have no part in it, for it will not be founded on laws which issue from the brain of man, but upon laws which are of one origin with those that govern the physical world. Of them Quesnay, one of the fathers of Political Economy, has said, "These Laws of the Physical World were ordained for good alone, and there must be no attribution to them of ills which are the just and inevitable penalty for their violation."

PART I

THE STATE OF WAR

CHAPTER I

FORMATION OF PRIMITIVE COMMUNITIES AND THE CONDITIONS NECESSARY TO THEIR EXISTENCE

THE formation of primitive communities has been ascribed to a peculiar feeling in man of sympathy towards his kind, but more careful observation proves that humanity owns no such innate sentiment. The appearance of such a feeling results from a need for mutual support, and from the interests evoked by this need. A community of interests and needs is the foundation of human friendship, while the opposition of needs and interests is not only capable of provoking antipathy, but it is notorious that nothing on earth has the same power of moving a man to violent

The Society of To-morrow

and implacable hatred as a member of his own species. Human associations were, in fact, the product of simple necessity. Thus, and only thus, could man realise pleasures and avoid sufferings which he must otherwise have been satisfied to imagine or endure.

When, on the other hand, any living creature was best adapted to a solitary existence, it adopted this mode of life, as do the carnivoræ. The need of mutual assistance led other orders to a gregarious habit, and human society was originated in this way. Social life imposed itself upon men as the one means to their desired end—first in their duel with the beasts, of which they were at once competitors and a prey; later, when individual fought individual and tribe opposed tribe. The physically inferior unit, possessed of sufficient intelligence to make common cause with his like, was enabled to arbitrarily incline the balance, and survive for the profit of the race.

This first step led naturally to others, for the mere capacity to combine under actual threat of destruction by the more powerful was insufficient. The new confederacy had to learn the means of perpetuating itself, and how to organise and combine those means so as to yield the greatest obtainable power, whether for offence or defence.

Formation of Primitive Communities

Hence arose an organisation which can be traced through the most backward societies, and is visible, in a rudimentary form, even among the beasts. This is *government*.

A cursory survey of the conditions under which primitive societies were able to maintain their unity and to consolidate their forces, at once exhibits the part played by this organisation and the nature of its growth. These conditions can be summarised as the guarantee of internal and external security. In other words, those acts which are harmful to the community must be distinguished from those which are beneficial to it; the two categories must be clearly defined and maintained by a penalty as between man and man. An organisation intended to assure the integrity of the association—an integrity with which the welfare of each member was bound up—could only be formed by combining all individuals capable of discerning the opposition between the socially harmful and the socially profitable with those members, the individually strong, who were most capable of repressing such acts as were judged injurious to the body politic.

Doubtless the rules called laws, which distinguish the useful from the harmful, good from evil, are purely the fruit of observation and experience, and always more or less adapted to their purpose.

The Society of To-morrow

They are by so much the more valuable, so much the more "just," as they contribute more to the maintenance of the community by augmenting its strength. In any case they were, even from the first, a far better guarantee of their intended object than those individual rules to which they succeeded.

Similarly, however unjust or imperfect might be the government of an early state, it secured a greater security to the individual than he could ever have obtained for himself. In place of defending himself single-handed against those risks which were the common burden of each member, corporate protection became a personal right, while it was also secured at a far less proportionate cost. Before the advent of a "State" the isolated individual maintained a most precarious existence at the price of the major part of his time and labour. Henceforward much of that time and labour was set free, and the "member of a State" was enabled to expend it on the satisfaction of minor desires, or in the discovery of material, or the invention of instruments and processes, by which he at once obtained a greater return for his outlay and an increase of enjoyment or a diminution of suffering.

Members of one society are united by common

Formation of Primitive Communities

interest, whether it be mere personal security or the guarantee of their livelihood. This common interest naturally excites, and later develops, a feeling of sympathy between the associates, and next between them and the community. It embraces nothing beyond the limits of the association, horde, clan, or tribe. Individuals outside those limits, and the communities to which those individuals belong, are regarded with the scorn or hatred naturally due to a competitor in matters so vital. And competition between individuals or States is vital at this time, for until man has learned how to supplement the natural supply of the materials of subsistence his existence depends on that supply, and his own share can only be increased at the expense of a rival.

CHAPTER II

COMPETITION BETWEEN PRIMITIVE COMMUNITIES AND ITS RESULTS

As population began to outgrow the means of subsistence, which mankind had not yet learned to increase by artificial methods, primitive society was compelled to choose between the elimination of excess population, or the seizure of hunting grounds, or sources of agricultural supply, belonging to some neighbouring tribe. The strong again survived and the weak disappeared. But the new system of association was already securing a certain leisure and a degree of relief from the need for continuous effort. The more intelligent among the inferior powers seized their opportunity, and under the continual spur of the need of survival invented arms and methods of destruction which altered the natural balance of power. Victory inclined to their side, at least until the men of

Competition and its Results

sinews had learned to profit by their superior wisdom and to imitate their skill.

But a second result had occurred in the meanwhile. Engines of destruction were as useful in the field as in actual strife, and an improved art of war soon decreased the numbers of the wild animals. Here was a novel stimulus, at least for those tribes whose strength was insufficient to dispossess a neighbour. Habits of observation and the creative faculty, responding to the motive of need, realised that decisive step on the road of progress which, once and for all, lifted humanity beyond the regions of mere animalism. For the systematic destruction which he shared with the beasts, and which limited his numbers to the natural means of subsistence, man substituted the productive industries and, by acquiring the power of indefinitely expanding the means of subsistence, stood forth lord of creation.

Great nations, amply furnished with all that is needful for the maintenance of life, now succeed the tribes of a few hundred individuals which snatched a precarious existence from vast territories. But the identical causes which made their rise possible placed these nations face to face with a new peril. Every advance was accompanied by fresh danger at the hands of tribes still subsisting by war and the chase. The spectacle of their wealth was irresistibly attractive, and the prospects of a successful foray, as measured in the expectation of loot, became more and more desirable. Nations, on the other hand, depending upon agriculture and those arts of peace, whose creation accompanies the growth of industry applied to production of the material bases of life, lost their ancient aptitudes for the practices of war and the hunting field, if only because they ceased to use them.

In these unequal conditions civilisation must have perished in the bud had not the same process which determined the substitution of agriculture for the chase manifested itself anew. Instead of murdering and robbing, one nation imposed itself upon, and exploited, another. A raid is a temporary expedient, and the renewed harvests of violence yield a continually diminishing crop. Lands of plenty returned to the desert from which they had been wrested, for the toiler lay dead in his furrow. But no sooner did the more astute spoiler of his neighbour comprehend the position than he devised effective means for perpetuating his supply, and even for increasing its yield. Those who had previously ravaged now conquered the land to possess it; where they had

Competition and its Results

destroyed they enslaved, and the victim bought his survival by a surrender of the entire, or a part of, the nett profit of his labours.

The conqueror now became interested in protecting his sources of supply, and began to devise systems for the better exploitation of territories and of the populations which were enslaved. These systems are the first POLITICAL STATES, and their guarantee against further violation from outside was their subjection to those who had first seen the value of the new system. Thus was constituted a further pregnant advance, one whose natural process eventually guaranteed civilisation against the risks of destruction and a return to barbarism.

CHAPTER III

COMPETITION BETWEEN STATES IN PROCESS OF CIVILISATION

No sooner did the exploitation of conquered territory and subject populations become general, with the consequent rise of Political States—*of the States*—than the conquering communities became involved in two other forms of competition. Certain particularly warlike tribes persisted in the practices of destruction and of pillage, while the States, as between themselves, sought every possible means of expansion.

Like the founders and proprietors of any other business, the owners of a political State desired to increase the profits of the industry from which they obtained a livelihood. They might achieve this either by increasing the nett yields of their enterprise, the exploitation of subjects, or they could expand, win new territory, and, in consequence, new subjects. But the first method required a degree of progress which was not realisable in a day : the labour of their employés had to be rendered more productive by better administration and by improved methods of exploitation. An enlarged measure of liberty, and the enjoyment of an increased proportion of their own earnings, must also be secured to the workers. Now the absolutism of those who owned the States, sanctioned by right of appropriation and conquest, no less than by the overwhelming superiority of organised power, allowed them to use their subjects as mere chattels. Natural cupidity allotted to this " human cattle " no more than the mere necessaries of existence, often far less, and it was only long and costly experience of the loss caused by their own greed which forced statesmen to recognise that the surest and most efficacious means of enlarging their nett profit—whether taken in guise of forced labour or as taxes, in kind or in money—was to encourage the producer to increase his gross output.

To obtain new territory and more subjects was comparatively easy. It was a conception appealing naturally to the spirit and capacity of a conquering caste, and it appears, in every age and in all cases, as the first, often the sole, aim of their political system.

But there were latent consequences in this race

for territory and subjects to exploit, which the competitors never guessed. The owners of a State, liable to total, or partial, dispossession at the hands of a rival, maintained their position subject to neglecting none of the many activities which consolidate and guarantee the integrity of a political association. They had to learn that the perfection of the material, art, and personnel of armies, is of little value when unaccompanied by a similar development of political and civil institutions, of the fiscal and economic systems.

Everywhere and in every age, it is this form of competition which stimulated men to perfect the institutions of politics and war, of the civil, fiscal, and economic State. Always and in all ages, also, the more progressive communities—those which develop their destructive and productive institutions to the highest degree—become the strongest and win the race. Our earlier volumes have seen this process at work. We have seen that improved agents of destruction advance production by continually enlarging its outlets. The security of civilisation has been assured neither by the arts of peace nor yet by those of war, but by the co-operation of both.[1]

[1] See the author's "l'Evolution Economique du XIXme Siècle," and also "l'Evolution Politique et la Révolution."

CHAPTER IV

DECLINE OF DESTRUCTIVE COMPETITION

SINCE profit is the motive of war no less than of all other human actions, an alliance between the arts of production and destruction soon lessened the inducement which prompted tribes to live by pillage and violence alone. Raiding a civilised community became less and less profitable as the art and *matériel* of war came to require a moral force, an amount of knowledge and capital, which only civilisation can command. Expeditions, undertaken for the sake of pure pillage, therefore ceased to return those enormous profits which had made them the favourite occupation of barbarian hordes. Tribal incursions tend to bring no profit, or to secure such hazardous and unsatisfactory returns that what was hitherto a rule becomes increasingly rare, occurs only on the most distant and least guarded frontiers, and is finally abandoned. Then the old order is reversed, for the civilised State becomes the aggressor, subdues the barbarian, and occupies his place. This expansion of civilisation at the expense of the uncivilised began many centuries ago, and when its motive is naturally exhausted—probably within the present century—the cause of many wars will have passed away.

Indeed wars, undertaken on this account, are already of secondary importance, since they seldom call for the exercise of more than a most insignificant portion of the resources of a State. It is when State meets State that the full power of modern military equipments is seen, and these occasions are the grand motive of their establishment. So immense and so costly is this apparatus that there is scarcely a State which does not expend upon its upkeep more treasure, more labour, and even more intelligence, than is allotted to any productive industry, agriculture alone excepted.

It has always been difficult to define the actual profits derived from a war, but, until the integrity of civilisation was finally ensured from barbarian aggression, these profits were of two kinds. Every conqueror in war is rewarded with material gains and moral satisfaction, but victory in those times likewise secured a higher degree of security. This

Decline of Destructive Competition

better security of civilisation was the measure of its advance in the arts of war, for war was its sole possible criterion.

Whether moral or material, the gains of war have always been practically monopolised by the proprietary and governing element within the victorious State. These profits were never so high as when conquest was followed by a partition of the newly conquered territory and its inhabitants, for the victors thus gained an extra glory and prestige—over and above the common glory of victory—in that they had escaped the fate which they now meted out to the vanquished. Meanwhile, their victory had also screened their own slaves, serfs, or subjects, from the ills of a possible invasion, with its inevitable change of masters, of whom the new were often the more brutal and rapacious. Finally, every war which resulted in an advance, however feeble, in the art of destruction, marked the achievement of one more step upon the long road of that progress whose goal was the establishment of civilisation.

But, as victory ceased to be synonymous with the act of massacring the vanquished, even of enslaving them, these several profits diminished. The defeat of a State now entails little more than a nominal alteration in the quarter to which allegiance is owed. Also, since the safety of civilisation is established, the profits derived from a war no longer include this count. But such profits as do remain are the perquisite of the governing power in the State, and they are shared between the military and the civil arms. A war benefits the military hierarchy by accelerating advancement in grade and pay; by those extraordinary "votes," or honorariums, which a grateful nation accords to successful leaders; and by the glory acquired, although this has diminished in value with the constant diminution in the damages and dangers from which victory saves a nation, and the benefits which it bestows. A successful war benefits the politician by increasing his power and influence, but it cannot be said to appreciably affect the precarious tenure of his office.

A war—such wars at least as enlarge the national boundaries—brings profit to a third class in the State, the officials, for it enlarges the scope of their activities. But it must be confessed that profit of this kind tends to be somewhat temporary, for it is certain that the new territory must ultimately produce its own aspirants to administrative positions, who will dispute the field with the subjects of the conquering State. Finally,

Decline of Destructive Competition

profit is sometimes taken in the form of a monetary indemnity in place of actual territorial aggrandizement. Such an indemnity is usually devoted to repairing the inevitable waste and damage of war, or to enlarging the victor's armaments.

But, besides winning profits for the victor, every war occasions loss and injury to the masses who are engaged in the productive industries, and these evils are felt by the subjects of neutral States no less than the subjects of actual belligerents. The very transformation which has been effected in the machinery of destruction has likewise increased the sphere of its effects, and the gravity of the ills which it entails.

The direct losses of war are those of life and capital, and these losses have grown side by side with that increase of power which has followed the growth of population, of wealth, and of credit, particularly among the States of the Old World and in the course of the last century. Nor is loss of life felt less directly than losses of capital, for it is the physical flower of a population which enters the army, and their destruction entails the perpetuation of a less effective type. Direct loss of this kind primarily affects the combatants, the area of indirect damage follows the extension of international interests. Markets are curtailed, the bulk of exchanges is diminished, the demand for capital and labour is arrested. In fact, while expenditure is suddenly increased, a check is put upon the action of those agencies which supply the means, nor are these losses and damages counterbalanced by any corresponding augmentation of the general security.

But, worst burden of all, the persistency of war obliges every nation to maintain a vast permanent machinery of destruction, and every progress in the art or science of war now augments the cost of this establishment.

Every State must keep pace with the armaments of its neighbours. It must, in the very midst of peace, devote a continually increasing proportion of revenue to maintaining the race of the present and redeeming the debts of the past. Nor is this all. More and more men are taken from the ranks of industry and consigned to a life of idleness and demoralisation, until, or in case, it may be necessary to employ them in the work of destruction.

Having accomplished its natural task of assuring security, war has now become harmful. We shall see that it is doomed to give place to a higher form of competition—productive or industrial competition.

CHAPTER V

WHY THE STATE OF WAR CONTINUES WHEN IT NO LONGER FULFILS A PURPOSE

WAR has ceased to be productive of security, but the masses, whose existence depends upon the industries of production, are compelled to pay its costs and suffer its losses without either receiving compensation or possessing means to end the contradiction. Governments do possess this power, but if the interests of governments ultimately coincide with the interests of the governed they are, in the first instance, opposed to them.

Governments are enterprises—in commercial language, "*concerns*"—which produce certain services, the chief of which are internal and external security. The directors of these enterprises—the civil and military chiefs and their staffs—are naturally interested in their aggrandizement on account of the material and moral benefits which such aggrandizement secures to themselves. Their home policy is therefore to augment their own functions within the State by arrogating ground properly belonging to other enterprises; abroad they enlarge their domination by a policy of territorial expansion. It is nothing to them if these undertakings do not prove remunerative, since all costs, whether of their services or of their conquests, are borne by the nations which they direct.

If, now, we consider a nation as the consumer of what its government produces, we see that it is to the interest of the governed to take from government only such services as the latter is able to produce better and at a less cost than other enterprises, and to purchase what it takes at the lowest possible price. Similarly, a nation requires that an annexation of territory should result in such an enlargement of its markets as will be sufficient to enable it to recover all the costs of acquisition, besides a profit; and this profit must not be less than the returns which could have been secured by any other employment of its capital and labour.

But this relation of government and nation, as producer and consumer, is not a free market. Government imposes its services, and the nation

Why the State of War Continues

has no choice but acceptance. Certain nations, however, possess constitutional governments, and these nations have a right of assent and of arranging the price. But despite the reforms and revolutions which have been so frequent during the last hundred years, this right has altogether failed to establish an equilibrium between the positions of consumer and purveyor of public services. More, the governments of to-day are less interested than were their forerunners to refrain from abusing the powers and resources of their nations, while the nations are also less interested in, and perhaps less capable of, guarding against such abuse.

Under the old system the political establishment, or the State, was the perpetual property of that association of strong men who had founded, or conquered, it. The members of this association, from the head downwards, succeeded by hereditary prescription to that part of the common territory which had fallen to their share at the original partition, and to the exercise of those functions which were attached to their several holdings. Sentiments of family and property, the strongest incentives known to the human race, combined to influence their action. They desired to leave to their descendants a heritage which should be neither less in extent nor inferior in condition to that which they had received from their fathers, and to maintain this ideal the power and resources of the State must be increased, or at least maintained in all their integrity. There was also a fiscal limit to the imposts which they exacted from their subjects, any overstepping of which involved personal loss, often personal danger. If they abused their sovereign power as possessors, whether by exhausting the taxable potentiality of the population or by squandering the product of an impost which had become excessive, their State fell into poverty and decay, and they themselves lay at the mercy of rivals who were only too alert and ready to seize any opportunity of enrichment at the expense of the decadent or defenceless. The governed were able to check any abuse of sovereign power on the part of government through the pressure which was exerted on the ruler by his hope of transmitting his power to his children, and by that form of competition which constituted the State of War.

Meanwhile, as external dangers decreased and a continual evolution in the machinery of warfare required yet larger expenditure, competition ceased to exert continuous pressure. Hence the measure of its stimulus declined. But at the same

Why the State of War Continues

time the masters of States abated nothing of those imposts and services which they exacted from their subjects, but without the previous justification of danger. Hence a growing discontent sprang up in those classes whose power had advanced with their progress in the arts of industry and commerce, and this process continued until it resulted in the fall of the old order.

The chief feature which distinguishes the new order and separates it, in theory at least, from that which preceded it, is the transfer of the political establishment, of *the State*, to the people themselves. With it, naturally, passed that sovereign power which is inseparable from ownership of the domain and the subjects of the State. This power which was exercised by the chief, generally hereditary, of the government of the political association, and which included a power of absolute disposition over the lives and goods of subjects, was justified by the original State of War. Under the conditions which then prevailed it was essential that the chief who was responsible for the safety of a State should have unlimited powers to requisition the person and resources of every individual, and to use them in any way which he might judge good, whether for actual defence of the State or for the purpose of increasing its resources by territorial expansion. The ownership of the political establishment might pass into the hands of the nation, but the need for such a power remained. Just as long as the State of War was the dispensation which regulated the world, so long was a power of unlimited disposition over the individual, his life and goods, an essential attribute of governments responsible for national security.

But as experience had already shown how liable this delegation of the sovereign power was to abuse, it was necessary to devise measures which should ensure its proper exercise. Also, as experience showed that the nation was not able to fulfil the office of ruling itself, the theorists responsible for erecting the new order withdrew from it all powers beyond that of nominating those delegates to whom the exercise of sovereign power was to be entrusted. Such delegation involved the risk of unfaithful service on the part of those who were chosen, and it was also foreseen that discrepancies might arise between their policy and the national will, if for no other reason than their too long maintenance in power. A more or less restricted period was therefore placed upon their mandate.

Why the State of War Continues

Experience also foreshadowed another difficulty. Delegates are no more capable than their constituents of fulfilling the whole office of a government. It is not possible that they should organise, carry on the necessary machinery for guaranteeing external and internal security, and fulfil those other duties which, rightly or wrongly, are required of "government." The new "constitutions," then, limited the sovereign power delegated to government to the exercise of the legislative prerogative, with a further right of deputing the executive power to ministers who should be responsible to it and who should be compelled to conform their conduct, under penalty of dismissal, to the will of a majority in the assembly of delegates.

This method of dividing the sovereign power among various executive agencies was capable of many variations. In a constitutional monarchy the chief office in the State remained subject to hereditary transmission, but its occupant was declared irresponsible and his action was limited to the sole function of nominating, as responsible minister, the man chosen by the majority of the national representatives. These representatives are nominally chosen by the nation, by those members of the nation who possess political rights, but in point of fact they are no more than the nominees of associations, or *parties*, who contend for the position of "State-conductors" on account of the material and moral benefits which accompany the position.

These associations, or political parties, are actual armies which have been trained to pursue power; their immediate objective is to so increase the number of their adherents as to control an electoral majority. Influential electors are for this purpose promised such or such share in the profits which will follow success, but such promises—generally place or privilege—are redeemable only by a multiplication of "places," which involves a corresponding increase of national enterprises, whether of war or of peace. It is nothing to a politician that the result is increased charges and heavier drains on the vital energy of the people. The unceasing competition under which they labour, first in their efforts to secure office, and next to maintain their position, compels them to make party interest their sole care, and they are in no position to consider whether this personal and immediate interest is in harmony with the general and permanent good of the nation. Thus the theorists of the new order, by substituting temporary for permanent attribution of the

Why the State of War Continues

sovereign power, aggravated the opposition of interests which it was their pretended purpose to co-ordinate. They also weakened, if they did not actually destroy, the sole agency which has any real power to restrain governments, in their capacity of producers of public services, from an abuse of the sovereign power to the detriment of those who consume those services.

The constitutions were, nevertheless, lavish in their promise of guarantees against this possibility, the most notable of which has, perhaps, been the power of censure vested in the press—a right which has too often proved quite barren of result. For the press has found it more profitable to place its voice at the disposal of class or party interests and to echo the passions of the moment rather than to sound the voice of reason. Nowhere has it been known to act as a curb on the governmental tendency to increase national expenditure.

Economic reasons, the advances of industry and expansion of credit, have actively furthered the same tendency. During last century industrial activity increased by leaps and bounds, and the continual advance in the wealth of nations enabled them to support charges which would have crushed any other age. The development of public credit has also provided a device by which posterity has been burdened with a continually increasing proportion of the expenditure of to-day, and, in particular the costs of war have been almost entirely defrayed thus. Nor is this all. The present generation, or at least an important and influential part of it, has been interested in the system of spending borrowed money, since they reap the entire profits which result from the consequent increase in business, but are only required to furnish a mere fraction of the funds which must ultimately redeem these liabilities.

This is the true reason why that sovereign power, which is still the attribution of government, has increased the liabilities of nations to a far greater extent than was ever known under the old order. And it has done this no less by enlarging its functions in a manner utterly contrary to sound economics, than by continuing a system of wars which are no longer justified as in any way promoting the security of civilisation.

CHAPTER VI

CONSEQUENCES OF THE PERPETUATION OF THE STATE OF WAR

As long as war was the necessary guarantee of security—a guarantee whose failure must have continually reduced human societies to a state akin to mere animalism—the sacrifices which it entailed, and the losses which it caused, were amply compensated by its contribution towards the permanence of civilisation. But this compensation has ceased to exist since the powers of destruction and production, attained under its impulse, assured a decisive preponderance to the civilised nations. More, the very progress of which war was the prime agent has increased its burden. Modern war entails a greater expenditure of life and capital, and, directly or indirectly, greater damage. And even if it is impossible to calculate the sum of these losses and this expense, we can obtain some idea of their bulk by a summary survey.

The Society of To-morrow

We need do little more than note a few figures. The various States of Europe have accumulated a debt of 130 milliards of francs (£5,200,000,000), of which the goodly sum of 110 milliards (£4,400,000,000) was added during last century. Practically the whole of this colossal total was incurred on account of wars. The army of these same nations numbers more than 4,000,000 men in time of peace; on a war footing it reaches 12,000,000. Two-thirds of their combined budgets are devoted to the service of this debt, and to the maintenance of their armed forces by sea and land. When we turn to the rate at which public charges have increased during the century, we find that the total monetary contribution has advanced 400 or 500 per cent., and that the "blood-drain" among Continental nations has followed on an almost identical scale.

In the particular case of France, the budget now stands at four milliards of francs (£160,000,000) as against one at the time of the Restoration; during the same period the figure of the annual conscription for the army has been increased from 40,000 to 160,000 men. Other States have suffered a very similar addition to their burdens, and in every case the second half of the nineteenth century was marked by a higher rate of increase.

Consequences of the State of War

It is true that the population of Europe has doubled since the year 1800, and that the marvellous inventions which have revolutionised every branch of productive industry have enlarged its productive capacity to an even greater extent. Hence, although available statistics are admittedly faulty, we may allow that productive capacity has developed concurrently with the exactions on output. The rate of taxation continues to rise, but there are signs that the rate of industrial production is beginning to flag. When, as of late, the figures of the birth rate, of general commercial circulation, and of the yield of taxation, exhibit a considerable slackening, it is clear proof that the general production of wealth is suffering a check. Meanwhile the causes which govern an advanced scale of imposts exhibit no retrogressive tendencies, and there are no grounds for supposing that the State of War will, in the twentieth century, fail to maintain a rate of advance at least equal to that shown in the nineteenth.

It is, therefore, a question whether the taxes which have met that expenditure, and the service of those debts, will continue to suffice. If, for example, France cannot support a budget of eight milliards of francs (£320,000,000), and the service of a debt of sixty milliards (£2,400,000,000) upon her present taxes, the deficit must be made good by an increase in their assessment or the imposition of new imposts. But the laws of fiscal equilibrium set a strict limit to the degree within which it is possible to impose new taxes, or to increase the rates of those already in force. The relative productivity of taxes soon shows when this point has been overstepped, for then returns not only cease to rise, but immediately begin to fall. A continuance of the State of War therefore, means that a moment will come when the governing class will, itself, be stricken at the very sources of its means of subsistence.

But the growing burdens of military expenditure are not the only trouble imposed by a continuance of this system. Equally injurious is the necessity which it entails of continuing to endow governments with a sovereign power of disposition over the life and property of the subject. War acknowledges no limit to the sacrifices which it may demand of a nation, and governments must necessarily have an equal power of compelling those sacrifices. The hereditary chief of the oligarchy, which owned the political organisation under the old system, possessed this power absolutely. The new order theoretically transferred it to the nation, but its practical exercise was in-

Introduction

injurious to the workers; because hitherto it has produced nothing but the oppression of the weak by the strong; because it has led to disastrous crises wherein millions have been ruined or have perished; because liberty without control is Anarchy." I reply, however, that you have to prove that the evils you attribute to liberty, or to what I call "free competition," have not their origin in monopoly, in undue restrictions.'"

What M. de Molinari desires to do is to set forth, with abundance of illustration, the fact that what human society needs is no such all-embracing organisation of industry and commerce as socialists desire, but a *régime* of absolute liberty, a fair field and no favour; and that this has hitherto been impeded by the despotism and interference of the State, the existence of powerful military and official classes whose personal interests are bound up with militarism, conquest, and war. What he writes under this last head is of the utmost value, and will strengthen the hands of those engaged in the crusade of Peace. His demonstration of the certain ruin impending over the most civilised states, in consequence of vast and growing military expenditure and the policy of annexation, is convincing, and deserves universal attention. It is to this state of things that he, of course, attributes the serious financial and economic condition of European nations; and he sees that it is indispensable to put an end to

Consequences of the State of War

vested in the leaders of the party in temporary and precarious possession of office. We have already seen that this transfer resulted in increased abuse of the sovereign power, and that all guarantees erected for the protection of the individual proved ineffectual. Whatever the intentions of a government, its tenure of office is so uncertain that party interest must be its first care.

Rulers, under the old system, had only to consider an oligarchy in hereditary possession of the superior political functions, military and civil. If this oligarchy condescended to inferior functions, much more to the servile practices of industrial and commercial life, it abdicated its position. Its demands on government were exacting, but were confined within narrow natural limits. High office was hereditary in a few families, and the sovereign's obligations were fulfilled when he had satisfied their ambition and cupidity. Modern government has to satisfy a vastly greater number of equally hungry suitors. Whereas it was sufficient to find honourable positions and sinecures for the members of the few families which constituted the oligarchy, a modern State has to satisfy thousands, one may say hundreds of thousands of families, all possessed of political power and influence. These men seek

The Society of To-morrow

every kind of place, and press every kind of interest, and can only be satisfied at the expense of the rest of the nation. Policy and protection —of certain classes or certain interests—are added to militaryism as burdens of the body politic. These charges on production, shared by the State and its *protégés*, may be added to, or subtracted from, the share of the actual agents of production—capital and labour. They are added when the producer is enabled to increase the price of his product by the entire sum of the tax, as occurs when a country protects a home product from the competition of other countries whose producers are less burdened. The impost is, in this case, paid by the consumer, and—whether derived from invested capital or from direct labour—the purchasing power of his income is correspondingly diminished. The manufacturer is, however, a consumer, and also—in that capacity —a sufferer from the results of a protective duty. But the manufacturer of a protected article—and his sleeping partners, if he have them—is usually able to obtain advantages which more than balance his decreased capacity of consumption. The combined burdens of tax and impost duty therefore fall upon the masses, the men whose labours are unprotected.

Consequences of the State of War

External competition sometimes prevents producers from increasing the price of their product by the full amount of a protective duty. The share of profits claimed by the State must, in this case, be subtracted from the shares of the agents of production. As the burden of taxation is rising at a practically concurrent rate among all nations, this case may be considered exceptional.

The nature of capital saves it from this deduction from the shares of the agents of production. Capital is itself a fruit of production, and production is only an incidental of its real intention. Capital is formed as an insurance against the eventualities of life, and suffers no diminution from an indefinite existence. It becomes productive—is applied to productive purposes, only when such application yields a sufficient return to cover the privation consequent on such employment, to counterbalance the accompanying risk, and to provide a profit. When returns do not cover this deprivation, risk, and profit, capital is withdrawn from, or ceases to enter, the field of production. Government can reduce the spheres open to capital by imposing burdens upon those spheres, but it has no power of reducing the rate of profit necessary to bring capital into the field of production.

The Society of To-morrow

Labour—the second agent of production—has no such power of self-protection. It must employ itself in production or lack the immediate necessities of subsistence. Unless it can emigrate to countries less burdened—always a difficult and costly operation—the share of labour is mulcted to supply the demands of government and its *protégés*. It is this increasing deduction [by the State] from the share of labour in the fruits of production, which socialists attribute to capital. They maintain that the remuneration of labour has not risen in proper proportion to the enormously increased returns of production, because capital has used its power to seize most, if not all, of the rightful dues of the worker. They have therefore stirred up strife between the two essential factors of production—an action which inevitably aggravates all that it pretends to cure.

Labour does suffer from grave ills, but so far are these from being solely due to insufficient remuneration that the worker has, in many cases, only to thank his own incapacity for the right conduct of life. Faults in the administration of the State are aggravated by the evils in individual self-government : the former do not cause the latter, but they do hinder their cure.

The sovereign power of governments over the

Consequences of the State of War

life and property of the individual is, in fact, the sole fount and spring of militaryism, policy, and protection. The rationale of the survival of this power is that we still live in a State of War, and the abolishment of that "state" is the present, most urgent, need of society. The solution is natural and inevitable, since the new conditions of social existence daily become more incompatible with its continuance. But, meanwhile, we can hasten the impulse, and so hasten likewise the realisation of that progress which the State of Peace will render possible.[1]

[1] This subject will be found, more fully developed, in the author's "Grandeur et Décadence de la Guerre."

PART II

THE STATE OF PEACE

CHAPTER I

THE COLLECTIVE GUARANTEE OF THE SECURITY OF NATIONS

A permanent State of Peace among all civilised nations may be assured by substituting their collective guarantee of external security for the present system, by which each State is its own guarantor. The cost of this superannuated system is enormous and constantly rising, while its total inability to guarantee the weak against the strong furnishes convincing proof that the moment cannot be long deferred before this momentous change forces its own acceptance. Taught by an identical need, primitive society long ago learned how to establish a collective assurance of the security of the individual horde, clan, or tribe. Man, in isolation, had expended

Guarantee of the Security of Nations

the greater part of his time in obtaining subsistence and defending himself from attack. He had, therefore, bought those services at the highest price, but association at once reduced their cost. The collective guarantee continued to demand considerable exertions on the part of each associate, but there was a clear saving both of time and effort, and the resultant security was incomparably greater than anything yet obtained by individual exertion.

A mutual assurance of this kind succeeded on one condition. The individual must cede the right of judgment to the association, in all cases where interest or temper brought him into conflict with a fellow-member; and the verdict must be executed by State agency alone. Whether directly exercised, or delegated to an executive acting *in nomine Societatis*, the judgment of the community replaced that of the individual. The judgment was always enforced by an irresistible power, while a code of laws—the necessary consequent of the change—defined the rights of each associate, and established the penalties for breach, or attempted breach, of these rights. The severity of penalties was graduated according to the gravity of the offence committed or the degree of damage caused by the attempt.

The Society of To-morrow

However imperfect collective justice was, and still is, it has always, and in all cases, proved superior to the individual system. Experience attests the absolute incapacity of man for equitable judgment, when his own interests are at stake. Interest or passion paralyses the capacity for right judgment, and leads men to maintain the most unfounded pretensions. Such a judge executes his own verdict, and no matter how far it is the fruit of blind impulse, instinct, or appetite, nor how obviously all right may be upon the other side, its execution is solely a matter of relative personal strength. While each man is a law unto himself judgment is invariably subordinated to interest and its execution to the rule that "right is might."

National differences are subject to identical influences. Each nation claims to be in the right, and if a sense of justice compels any members of the State to admit that there is reason in the claims of an adversary, the multitude blinded by passion, or the politician lusting after popularity, forthwith denounces them as traitors. When such differences are put to the arbitrament of war, individuals, on either side, condemning the injustice of a judgment passed under the influence of passion or interest, must either join in a

Guarantee of the Security of Nations

struggle which their hearts condemn, or dare—and few have the courage—to disown their country rather than be parties to an unjust act. And finally, between nations as between individuals, the victory is to the strong without regard to abstract right.

In face of the fact that the cost of such autonomy increases every day, is it profitable that each nation shall remain judge, and executor of judgment, in causes affecting its own interests? Improved communications and the enormously extended area of security, have multiplied international interests and with them occasions of conflict. Undreamed-of improvements in the processes and machinery of production have, on the other hand, increased the returns of productive industry, and with them the ability to support a continually growing outlay upon destructive armaments. With augmented opportunity for differences with adversaries whose power was always growing, compelled to have recourse to arms whenever they supposed, rightly or wrongly, that justice was on their side, nations have been allowed no alternative but to incessantly renew and enlarge the apparatus for supporting their judgments. The army and navy have, without doubt, offered careers to certain sections

The Society of To-morrow

within the nation, and these have encouraged their development for purely selfish reasons. But the multitude, on whom the burden of maintenance falls, has no opportunity of enforcing moderation; armaments are the guarantee of their security. No nation willingly condemns itself, in case of a conflict, to lying at the mercy of its foe for lack of the means of defence, and whatever the injustice or degree of the injury to which it is exposed; neither will it willingly contemplate the fact that, if a war arise, the battle must be fought with insufficient or superannuated arms, and with no better hope than to defer the hour of surrender. If it be only for honour's sake, it must defend its rights, and it will place this interest before every other. Civilised nations have, thus, been driven to increase their powers for destruction concurrently with, and even to a higher degree than, their progress in production. And in Europe, where international interests are peculiarly complex, and each nation stands shoulder to shoulder with its rivals, the peoples are now bowed beneath the load of armed peace.

It may be argued that they have at least preserved the right to judge their own cause and to execute that verdict. But this right—daily bought more dearly—is now only partially

Guarantee of the Security of Nations

existent, and, even in that degree, is enjoyed by none but the strongest. The minor States of Europe expend, proportionately, quite as much as the larger, but, if their right of autonomous judgment has survived, not even themselves will suggest that they are free to attempt its execution. What has been called the Concert of Europe—an association of all the greater States—has arrogated to itself not only the right of hindering or arresting such attempts, but even of modifying or entirely reversing their terms.

This association of the Great Powers, with its self-constituted claims to a right of intervention between independent sovereign States with the avowed purpose of preventing them from executing their individual judgments, has naturally justified its action by some pretension. The pretension is one of a right superior to that of any individual State—the right of civilisation to interdict any act injurious to the community. Such a claim emphasises a new factor in the growing solidarity of interests brought about by industrial progress, and an extended international market. While external economic and financial relations were of no great importance, and the effects of war largely local, neutrals scarcely felt the reaction consequent on a struggle, and this tie

The Society of To-morrow

remained dormant. But the situation altered so soon as the innumerable connections of a world-commerce sprang into existence. The smallest modern war affects neutral interests as certainly as those of the actual belligerents. From this right, inevitable under the circumstances, sprang the right of neutral powers to intervene and compel the reference of disputes to a less violent arbitrament. Great States exercised it upon such of their neighbours as were too weak to resent the interference. The right of every independent State to judge its own cause, and execute its own judgment, was destroyed or limited in this way, and the smaller State was, in point of right, placed in an inferior position to that of its more powerful neighbour.

The smaller States were, naturally, not slow to feel the indignity, but possessed small ability to revolt. An appeal to their prescriptive right to use the judgment of battle entailed injury to all nations. Those nations had their own right to prevent this injury, and to claim indemnity in case of its commission. Debarred from individual exercise of their right of sovereignty, the smaller States may justifiably demand a share in the collective right which the greater States have arrogated to themselves, and to be admitted to

Guarantee of the Security of Nations

the Concert of Europe in the position to which their relative size entitles them.

It is not difficult to forecast the probable results of such a step, and the step will be realised so soon as the burden of a continued State of War, and the crushing costs of the armaments which it entails, shall have become too intolerable.

Whether the tie were one of compulsion or founded on a voluntary basis, an association of all the States of Europe, with the States of other quarters of the globe, must command superior powers to those of any member of the confederacy. Such a confederacy could compel any member to submit all quarrels to some form of systematic arbitration, and the verdicts of such a tribunal would be sanctioned by irresistible force. Disarmament would then follow as inevitably as the feudal lords abolished their private armies when confronted with an Emperor, chief, or King invested with the exercise of sovereign power and controlling the entire forces of the nation. Each State would reduce its armaments to the exact point necessary to enable it to fulfil their remaining purpose—to fulfil the duties of a guarantor of the common security against attack by peoples still outside civilisation. The proportion of these nations is

The Society of To-morrow

so small that the force necessary for this task could be reduced within limits similar to those of the apparatus maintaining the internal security of States, since the right of individual justice has been superseded by a system of State-justice vested in an authority emanating from the national entity.

The savings to be effected by a cessation of a State of War will be apparent, however cursory has been our glance at the consequences which it entails—the grinding costs under which nations labour, and the losses, directly or indirectly, originated by it. But this economy in blood and treasure will be no more than an incident of the benefits accompanying the advent of a State of Peace. A new cycle of progress will be opened, the era of a new and better life for humanity.[1]

[1] See Appendix, Note A—The Czar and Disarmament.

CHAPTER II

THE FREE CONSTITUTION OF NATIONALITY

THE first, and by no means least, advance which will follow the establishment of a State of Peace will be free constitution of nationality.

All history attests that it was force, and in no sense a voluntary agreement of both parties, which erected the associations called political States; and at this point it may be useful to recapitulate what we have already said on the subject. The strongest members of the species, usually hordes subsisting by the chase and pillage, seized the territories occupied by weaker members. The conquerors effected a partition of these lands, and compelled the inhabitants to work for their benefit, whether by reducing the conquered population to a state of slavery or by leaving them in possession of the land, but subject to a system of serfdom or of simple subjection. The origins of a political State were a commercial specu-

The Society of To-morrow

lation in agriculture or industry, and profits naturally depended upon the administrative capacity of their owner, the industry and productive aptitudes of the subject population, the fertility of the soil, and other similar conditions. Taken as forced labour, or as imposts in kind or in money, these profits constituted the owners' revenue, and were, as such, subject to no limitation but that of the entire nett production of which the labours of the slaves, serfs, or subjects were capable. On the one side these labours supported the proprietors of the enterprise—to-day we should call them shareholders—and, on the other, they paid for the defence and aggrandisement of the collective domain.

Every association which carries on an industrial business must devise an administrative system to direct its various services. The State was no exception to this rule. Like all other businesses, the State acknowledged no end but interest, and it identified this with the conservation and enlargement of its profits. But profits can only be increased in two ways. The yield of imposts, whether of labour, of kind, or in money, may be increased; or the area of production may be enlarged. The latter method was preferred by the associations which owned political "businesses," for the former required capacities for good government of which they were seldom possessed. But, since a community can only extend its domain at the cost of a neighbour, war naturally ensued, and while those communities which excelled in war enlarged their territory and their holdings in subjects, they increased their income at the same time. A merchant or manufacturer cares nothing for the race, language, or individual customs of his customers, and the States had no more regard for those of the persons who lived in the territories which they acquired. Their sole motive was interest, and all their actions were exclusively directed to obtaining those territories of which the conquest and maintenance seemed the most easy, and which promised the highest possibilities for lucrative exploitation. Entire populations, opposed in race, in language, and in customs, were thus drawn, whether they would or no, into the domain of the victorious association, to leave it only in accordance with the arbitrament of a new war, or according to family dispositions when a single house chanced to acquire complete sovereign control within the State.

To-day we consider such a method of constituting a nation, a nationality, or a "country,"

The Society of To-morrow

to be barbarous. But, in view of the diversity and inequality of the various species of the human race, and the conditions under which they originally existed, this method was not only the sole possible means, but it was also the sole effective method of preserving the more feeble varieties from extermination. If the strong had never found that it was more profitable to subject the weak—for the purpose of living permanently on the exploitation of their productive abilities—than to rob and massacre, as the Turcoman and Bedouin recently did; if they had not, for this reason, been interested in the survival of those races which were incapable of securing their own protection, civilisation could never have come to pass. It was the discovery that to protect the weak and to prey upon his industry offered higher profits than a systematic career of raiding which first established, and then perfected, the arts of industrial production. High, excessive even, as was the price at which the producer bought his security from the associations of strong men who appropriated him as slave, serf, or subject, there was still an exchange of benefits, and he also made a profit on the transaction.

This appropriation of the weak by the strong was absolute, and usefully so, since it induced the

Free Constitution of Nationality

proprietor to spare no effort in protecting his property. His rights as owner naturally extended to cession and exchange, however repugnant a change of masters might be to the feelings of "human property." Yet the change seldom affected status to any appreciable extent. Whether from indifference, or in the hope of attaching a new subject, conquerors voluntarily respected local institutions, and rarely attempted to place restrictions on the use of the indigenous language. They were content—and it was, indeed, the one thing needful to themselves—to collect the imposts, in money or in kind, which had been exacted by their predecessors. These taxes were seldom increased; occasionally, at all events for a time, they were reduced.

The modern conqueror is less liberal than his prototype in these respects, and it is a curious consideration that this retrogression in the treatment of conquered peoples has followed the extension to the same peoples of the rights enjoyed by their masters. The new *Theory of Sovereignty* places in the hands of the nation those rights of property in, and exploitation of, the State, which were heretofore a perquisite of the oligarchies, erected by "conquest" and led by a "house." But, by virtue of the same theory, the

The Society of To-morrow

nation has been declared "*one and indivisible*," so that the subjects, become sovereign, are no more free to sever their connection than before. Contrariwise, the nation is inseparable from the subjects, whom it may not sell or exchange; and if, under the compulsion of superior force, a nation is compelled to cede them, it is under immutable obligation to attempt their recovery on the first possible occasion.

From this theory of sovereignty have been derived two deductions which are, naturally, in absolute opposition. The first maintains that a population which has emerged from a state of subjection, and has acquired "ownership" of itself, cannot be separated from one nation and annexed to another without its own consent. This option was given to the Belgians when the armies of the Republic had conquered their territory, and it was also granted to the people of Savoy and Nice on their cession to France as a return for her services to the cause of Italian unity. The second, and contradictory, deduction—issuing this time from the theory of national indivisibility—refuses any right of secession from the State, and this refusal has been sanctioned by rigorous penalties, as if the right of accession to a State did not include the liberty of a withdrawal.

Free Constitution of Nationality

The United States interpreted the modern theory of sovereignty thus. The English Colonies voluntarily incorporated themselves in the Union, but when the Southern States desired to withdraw the Northern States compelled them to remain in it by force of arms. In point of fact, the liberty enjoyed by populations voluntarily annexed or united is limited to a right of changing the form of their subjection. They were subject to an oligarchy, personified in a more or less absolute king; they are now the subjects of a nation, whose mouthpiece is a constitutional or republican government. The individual subject enjoys the compensation of a share in the national sovereignty, but the degree, as may be imagined, is not large. In France it is one in thirty-eight million parts.

It may be disputed whether this infinitesimal share in the sovereign power is sufficient guarantee of individual rights, and even of the rights of particular groups. Government, more or less correctly invested with this delegated power, has imposed a uniform system upon the whole of the national domain. Under pretext of strengthening nationality by unifying it, no regard has been had to the diversity of the populations in the various regions, but the real reason for this

The Society of To-morrow

procedure was the wish to assure and facilitate, the exercise of sovereign rights.

In its most essential dispositions, at least, the old theory of sovereignty still maintains in such States as Germany and Russia. Even the meagre appearance of choice accorded under the new theory of sovereignty to populations which are annexed is denied to those which come into the relation with these States. Russia ignored the wishes of Poland when it annexed that country, and Germany appropriated Alsace-Lorraine with no inquiry as to their willingness to exchange French for German nationality. But, on the other hand, these governments of the old *régime* have found it profitable to borrow the practices of unification and assimilation initiated by their more advanced brethren. Populations annexed by them are deprived of their legislative and fiscal systems, and even of the national tongue. They are assimilated by the imposition of institutions which they dislike, and a language of which they are ignorant, while the conqueror never pauses to consider whether these despotic and brutal proceedings may not have a reverse effect to that which is intended, through the exasperation and repugnance which they induce, to assimilation and unification. And yet these means of State-

Free Constitution of Nationality

aggrandisement and national expansion, however offensive to those populations which are compelled, under the most grievous penalties, to transfer their love and faith from one nation to another, are still justified by the continuance of the State of War.

While that state continues nations must develop their powers of production and destruction to the greatest possible extent, or prepare to be engulfed at the next outbreak of war. They can enlarge those powers by either of two methods—territorial expansion or an augmentation of internal wealth and population. Territorial extensions are subject to this further rule, that the costs of acquisition and maintenance, incurred on account of the new territory, must not exceed the nett increase of revenue secured by the successful undertaking. Simple self-interest compels States to conquer more territory and to forbid secessions, for secession, besides entailing loss of land and income, may add those identical losses to the assets of a rival power. If Russia withdraws from Poland that country may join Prussia in a war against herself, and an independent Ireland might become the base of operations and supply for the invasion of England.

The State of War is in absolute opposition to the

The Society of To-morrow

right of free choice of nationality, of accession or secession. France solemnly proclaimed both rights. She permitted Belgium, Savoy, and Nice to exercise the former, but fenced their decisions with the most stringent guarantees. She denied all choice to Madagascar, Cochin-China, and the Arabs, and refuses to permit so much as a thought of withdrawal to territory that has once been subject to her flag. French territory, whether so for a long period or as a result of recent conquest, remains French unless lost by the fortunes of war.

A collective guarantee of peace would destroy this subservience to the State of War—a bondage which has appeared peculiarly intolerable since the case of Alsace-Lorraine. Such a guarantee would protect all States from aggression. Large or small, their integrity would be supported by a power superior to that of the most powerful partner, while every constituent part of a State would be free to vary its nationality at will or convenience. Secession could not menace the security of the remainder of a State, and could not therefore be opposed. The governing classes might not welcome the exercise of a right which curtailed their sphere of power, or, in the case of a composite nation, menaced their ability to favour numerically superior sections at the cost

Free Constitution of Nationality

of the less numerous. But such actions could no longer be justified by a plea that they served the predominant interest of national security, and public opinion would cease to support the claim.

The advent of a State of Peace will synchronise with a disappearance of internal troubles, caused by differences of race, custom, and language. Constituted voluntarily, and according to natural affinities, composed of sympathetic or homogeneous units under a system adapted to all idiosyncracies, nations will acquire the highest moral and material development of which they are capable. While the unity of States is maintained by force alone, sectional favouritism breeds divisions and hatreds. They will disappear when a community of interest and action, founded on a common choice of, and common love for, a fatherland freely chosen, is established as the sole and sufficient basis of nationality.

CHAPTER III

FREE CONSTITUTION OF GOVERNMENTS AND THEIR NATURAL FUNCTIONS

WE have seen that political sovereignty grew out of the right of property. Warlike societies seized a territory and its inhabitants for the purpose of founding a political State. The conquerors, become owners, used the lives and property of subjects according to their absolute will. To maintain States against the pressure of political and armed competition it was necessary to concentrate the rights of sovereignty. They became hereditary in the family of a chief, who might justifiably have used the words of Louis XIV., "*l'Etat c'est moi!*" This chief might grant his subjects certain rights, such as the rights of labour, exchange, and testamentary disposition; also certain guarantees of property and liberty. But permissions of this kind were entirely voluntary; he retained his owner's right of resumption. Moreover, he maintained absolute claims on life, liberty, and property to be used as, and whenever, required for the maintenance and welfare of the State. This supreme power—an attribute of sovereignty—has passed to the modern State, whose citizens delegate its exercise to government. Its original justification was the destruction, or dispossession, with which political and warlike competition continually menaced the proprietary association in each State. Conquest, to-day, implies little more than a nominal change of allegiance, and the damages which it inflicts are rather moral than material. But the right survives, though in a contracted form, and it will continue to exist while the nations are compelled to rely upon war as their sole guarantee against aggression, or the sole means of enforcing what each claims to be justice in cases of dispute.

But if security and rights are no longer weakened because a collective guarantee replaces the guarantee which each nation provided for itself, as the national assurance of protection has replaced the system of individual self-defence, the position is at once reversed, war ceases, and with it all need for that unlimited right of requisition over life, liberty, and property, which is the inevitable attribute of a government charged with maintaining national liberties during a State of War. Under the new order, the charges and services which the requirements of national security demand of the individual, will cease to be uncertain or contingent. They will become capable of valuation and a permanent assessment since they are :—

1. That every citizen shares in a guarantee of the civilised community against barbarian hordes or nations in an inferior state of civilisation, and outside the collective guarantee. But the extraordinary advances in the industries of production and destruction have given civilisation so great a prepotency that risks of this class are insignificant, and 100,000 men can easily maintain the frontiers of the civilised world against all attacks.

2. That every citizen helps to maintain a collective force, which shall be strong enough to execute the verdicts of international justice upon States refusing obedience, or attempting forcibly to maintain a personal estimate of right. A collective guarantee of the peace of nations entails absolute surrender, by each guarantor, of the rights of individual judgment and individual execution of judgment. This surrender was

long since imposed upon all subjects of a State, as the sole basis of social security, and it is universally observed except by the criminal and the duellist. Criminals break this obligation in blind obedience to the dictates of cupidity, or those other passions which are only capable of satisfaction at the expense of another. Duellists justify their default by denying the sufficiency of a collective justice in the case of certain personal offences. Society is usually content to ignore the duellist while carefully abstaining from any recognition of a claim which is in direct negation to its own; but it pursues the criminal so unceasingly that a numerically inconsiderable force of police is able to guarantee—though more or less imperfectly—individual life and property.

Civilised States could not be treated as criminals, but the instinct for war and a false idea of national honour might place nations in the relative position of duellists. The collective guarantee would intervene, at such a time, to enforce their renunciation of the right of personal justice, and to affirm the State of Peace. Every interposition of this kind would be a new demonstration of the irresistible power of the collective sanction, and the strongest member of the association must soon recognise its relative impotence. Then the guarantors may disband their contingent of armed forces, for public opinion will suffice to sanction the decrees of international justice. The guarantee of internal peace and external security will then only require an insignificant and constantly diminishing contribution from the members of the confederated States.

The primacy of national interest over all other claims ceases, at this point, to demand an absolute right of requisition over individual life, property, and liberty, so that it is possible to ascertain the exact and inviolable relation of individual and governmental rights. And we shall see that this adjustment will be fixed and determined by the nature of the public services and the conditions of their production.

Public services are the natural attributes of government, and are of two classes—general and local. General services are within the sphere of government proper; local services belong to provincial and local administrations.

The first duty of government is to ensure internal and external security to nation and citizen alike. Services proper to it differ essentially from those of the private association for they are *naturally collective.* Armies secure an entire nation from external aggression, and a police force exists for the equal benefit of all who inhabit the district which it serves. It is therefore no less necessary than just that all consumers of these naturally collective services should contribute to their cost in proportion to the service rendered and the benefit received. The failure of one consumer to bear his quota of the costs of such production reacts on the entire community, who are compelled to bear a proportion of his defalcations over and above their own contribution.

It seems almost superfluous to insist on the essential minority of naturally collective services. A police force serves every inhabitant of the districts in which it acts, but the mere establishment of a bakery does not appease their hunger. Bread, with all other victual, clothes, &c., are articles of naturally individual consumption; social security is an article of naturally collective consumption.

The substitution of a collective guarantee of peace for the individual action of each State must, consequently, restrict the number of functions, which are the natural and essential duty of government, to :—

The Society of To-morrow

A share in the common defensive apparatus protecting the association from external aggression;

A share in the machinery which guarantees internal peace within the association;

The provision of internal security within its own State, and the further performance of those services which are naturally and essentially collective.

CHAPTER IV

FREE CONSTITUTION OF GOVERNMENTS AND THEIR NATURAL FUNCTIONS (*continued*)

WE have now to examine the methods and conditions by, and under, which governments maintain international peace and establish internal security. As soon as nations emerge from their subservience to the State of War, and their constituent parts are free to form new groups or to erect autonomous States, the dangers of revolution and civil war, which are the fruit of compulsory union between heterogeneous and incompatible elements, will disappear together with the motives and pretexts previously used to justify appeals for external intervention. The "States Association" will only have to consider disputes and dissensions occurring between members, and it will refer these to tribunals maintained for the purpose. These tribunals will apply the same legal rules which govern the trial of actions and causes between individual litigants, and their verdicts will be enforced by the collective sanction of the association. Associated States will thus obtain external security by the best possible means, and at the least possible cost, while each will secure internal security under analogous conditions, and by a collateral system.

In order to be able to guarantee full security of person and property to the consumer, or —in case of damage suffered—a compensation in proportion to his loss, it is necessary that :—

(1) the producer impose certain penalties on those who commit offences against the person, or appropriate the property of others, and the consumer must agree to submit to these penalties, whenever he does a wrong to person or property ;

(2) the producer impose upon the consumer certain restrictions, designed to facilitate discovery of the authors of delicts ;

(3) the producer levy a regular contribution covering his costs of production plus the natural profit of his industry, each assessment to be graduated according to the consumer's position, the particular occupation in which he is en-

gaged, and the extent, nature, and value, of his property."[1]

It should be added that the consumer renounces his right of judging his own causes, and of executing his own judgments.

The production of internal security, therefore, necessitates a body of law—*a code*—specifying and defining wrongs against the person and property, with the penalties proper to each, and, further, other laws specifying the obligations and charges, which are no less necessary to enable their effective repression.

The execution of the laws, and the conditions accompanying the production of those services which are indispensable to the preservation of all society, further necessitate :—

(1) the institution of a judicial system, primarily adapted to a systematic discovery of the presumptive authors of delicts or crimes against the person or property, of determining guilt and innocence, and, in the case of those proved guilty, of executing the penalties set out in the code ; secondly, it must adjudicate upon actions and causes ;

(2) the institution of a police service entrusted

---

[1] Extract from " La Production de la Sécurite," *Journal des Economistes*, February 15, 1849 ; also printed in "Les Questions d'Economie Politique et de Droit Public," vol. ii. p. 245.

with the discovery and pursuit of the authors of delicts and crimes, and, in the second place, with executing the repressive penalties.

These are the constituent parts of an organisation producing internal security, and the conditions necessary to its effective action. A form of this essential organisation is found among the lowest races, but it remains notoriously imperfect even among the most civilised and most highly advanced States. Nor is a cause far to seek while the State of War continues to impose its conditions upon governments, the producers of security.

Invested with the exercise of the sovereign power attaching to the association which owned a conquered territory and its inhabitants, government owed this appropriated population no service—whether of affording security or otherwise — any more than a stock-owner owes a service to his sheep or cattle. Yet there was one difference between sheep or cattle and such a population. Whether appropriated by right of conquest, by hereditary devolution of territorial property, exchange, or purchase, such a population might rise against its masters. Plots might also grow up within the State, aimed at the deposition of the government of the proprietary association.

Free Constitution of Governments

Personal security, which it never distinguished from that of the State, commanded this government to make a first duty of precautions against this double peril. The initial step in this direction placed the judiciary and police system in dependence upon government, their first assigned duties being to repress attempts upon its supremacy, to discover the intrigues of rivals, and to supervise the actions, even the words, of malcontent subjects. The second measure of self-protection was to forbid the formation, without governmental sanction, of any association capable of serving as a dissentient or revolutionary centre, to retain control over authorised associations by setting a term to their duration, and to reserve a right of dissolution in every case. But, however constantly and largely preoccupied with personal security, government was compelled to afford some guarantees to individual life and property, since they are the foundation of all industrial progress, and revenue depends upon industry. That these duties were never more than a secondary care, more especially where a government's tenure of power was unstable, can be proved—if proof be needed—by the far greater severity of penalties guaranteeing the persons of those in power and of their agents, when compared with sanctions of the life and property of a citizen.

Fundamental changes might have been expected where the nations ceased to be owned by an association or a sovereign house. Governments, instituted or accepted by a nation—now self-owned — owed their nation those services for which it undertook the necessary charges and obligations. The government was, further, under obligation to increase the efficiency, and to reduce the cost, of those services. But a persistent State of War still compelled governments to value the security of the nation above that of the individual. The States continued to make advances in the industries of production and destruction, and, as each was a possible future combatant, the cost of national security rose continually. Under the new system, also, competition for the sovereign power was increased, and, while possession became more and more precarious, eager competitors were less scrupulous in the choice of means to attain it. Government, increasingly occupied with the problems of self-protection, relegated the protection of the subject to a still more secondary position. Finally, men who obtained power, or maintained it, by strictly legal means, were incessantly compelled to enlarge what may be termed

Free Constitution of Governments

the "political salaries fund," that is to say, the number of officials, and consequently the functions of the State. Ever occupied with the problem of national security, still more with the maintenance of their own power, further charged with a multiplicity of incongruous functions, modern governments can with difficulty fulfil their task. This is the real explanation of the grossly inadequate performance of their first duty—protection of the life and property of the individual.

But if a State of Peace were to succeed the State of War, if a collective guarantee secured the external security of nations; if, in consequence, nationality were the subject of free choice, and the sphere of governments limited to their natural attributions, competition would influence the production of this most essential service with results which must, to-day, appear chimerical. The first question to be solved on that day will be: "Is it more profitable for nations to produce their own security, or to contract for its production with a 'firm,' or company, possessing the necessary resources for, and the technical skill essential to, production of this kind?" Experience has long since demonstrated the economical inferiority of production by a monopolist governmental department. It is therefore probable that nations will prefer to contract, whether through agents or otherwise, with the "firm," or company, offering the most advantageous conditions for, and the most certain guarantees of, the supply of this article, which is one of naturally collective consumption.

Theoretically, at least, these conditions will only differ in one point from those of the present system, but this point is essential. The assurer must indemnify the assured—if attacked in life or property—in proportion to the damages suffered, without regard to the issue of any attempted recovery against the actual authors of the wrong.

Nor will such a system of indemnification be altogether new, since existing laws recognise a right to indemnity where a man has suffered in a riot. Civilised States assert the same principle in their claims for an indemnity to one of their subjects who has been injured, or to his family if he has been murdered, in the territory of an inferior power, or a power reputed inferior, although they are careful to refuse similar claims against themselves. The importance of this principle will be apparent when we consider how supremely effective it must be in inducing governments to perfect their machinery for discovering and repressing attacks on individual life and property.

Free Constitution of Governments

The conditions regulating the cost of security must differ in every country according to the prevalent standards of morality and civilisation, and similar differences in the obstacles to repressing crime. The assurer and the body of the assured will be jointly interested in maintaining an impartial and enlightened judiciary for adjudicating on crimes and delicts. Adam Smith has long since shown how competition solves this problem, and there can be little doubt that competition between fully independent judicial " companies " will hereafter repeat the same solution.[1]

[1] "The fees of court," says Adam Smith ("Wealth of Nations," Book V., chap. i., part 2), "seem originally to have been the principal support of the different courts of justice in England. Each court endeavoured to draw to itself as much business as it could, and was, on that account, willing to take cognisance of many suits which were not originally intended to fall under its jurisdiction. The Court of King's Bench, instituted for the trial of criminal causes only, took cognisance of civil suits; the plaintiff pretending that the defendant, in not doing him justice, had been guilty of some trespass or misdemeanour. The Court of Exchequer, instituted for the levying of the King's revenue, and for the enforcing payment of such debts only as were due to the King, took cognisance of all other contract debts; the plaintiff alleging that he could not pay the King, because the defendant would not pay him. In consequence of such fictions, it came, in many cases, to depend altogether upon the parties, before what court they would choose to have

their case tried; and each court endeavoured, by superior dispatch and impartiality, to draw to itself as many causes as it could. The present admirable constitution of the courts of justice in England was perhaps originally, in great measure, formed by this emulation, which anciently took place between their respective judges; each judge endeavouring to give, in his own court, the speediest and most effectual remedy which the law would admit, for every sort of injustice."

CHAPTER V

FREE CONSTITUTION OF GOVERNMENTS AND THEIR NATURAL FUNCTIONS (*continued*)

GOVERNMENTS, possessed, under the old system, of an unlimited power over the goods and persons of the subject, were naturally tempted to abuse this power for their own immediate advantage, or for that of the political and warlike society whose mandate they held. These motives might lead them to make large increases in the charges and obligations of the subject masses, but never to annex those industries which supported that body and consequently themselves. This was a natural consequence of the self-imposed limitation which confined the oligarchical owners of the State to the functions of government, military or civil. Their body had no motive for appropriating industrial occupations, at that period of human development both reputedly and actually inferior, but influenced government solely for the purpose of inducing armed acquisition of new territories and new subjects, consequently of increasing its peculiar spheres of activity. Hence governments of the old order seldom trespassed on the domain of private enterprise. If they did reserve a monopoly in certain classes of production—in the mintage of money, the manufacture of salt or tobacco—it was from purely fiscal considerations. Even these monopolies were not exercised directly, but farmed, with most other taxes, experience showing that a "farm" gave better returns than direct governmental monopolies.

The advance of production and trade consequent on extended security has changed this by erecting a numerous and powerful middle class, which claims a share in government, and has even obtained paramount influence in the more advanced States. The rivals for political office are chiefly recruited among the members of this class, and it has been observed that such of the old proprietary oligarchies as maintain a preponderance in their States, and continue to supply a majority in the personnel of the political, military, and administrative services, tend to a similar modification of interests, and to identify their cause with that of this middle class. The reason

Free Constitution of Governments

for this revolution is that progress which has reduced the emoluments of the proprietary class by enlarging the costs of war, reducing its frequency, and curtailing its profits. This loss compelled the class to seek compensation by increasing the returns derivable from landed property, and by undertaking functions hitherto despised. Political parties, containing members of both classes, could only obtain, and maintain, power by serving the actual or supposed interests of their constituents. The landed and industrial vote was purchased by protection and subvention—bounties—or by the provision of civil and military offices for such of its younger members as lacked the necessary character or energy to create a position for themselves. This is the explanation of those enormous and ever-increasing burdens with which militaryism, policy, and protection overwhelm the masses whose labour provides their cost.

If we now attempt to estimate the burden occasioned by the degree to which government has abused its unlimited power over individual life and property for the benefit of those classes on which it depends, an analysis of the budgets of most civilised States yields the startling fact that the two services of the army and the public debt absorb two-thirds of the entire revenue. A State of War does, doubtless, necessitate individual insurance against external aggressions, but the consequent premium seems altogether disproportionate to the risks assured. There can be small doubt that the enormous strength of European armies is due to the advantageous careers offered by the service to sons of influential aristocratic and middle-class families, or that the majority of the wars which have wasted the world for no good purpose during the past century were not undertaken at the mandate of the masses. Yet, willing or unwilling, it is they who furnish the necessary blood and treasure. Nor is this the only account. Society is heavily taxed in the increased costs which follow governmental appropriation of products and services naturally belonging to the sphere of private enterprise, such as posts, telephones, telegraphs, and railways. Add to this the price of a policy protecting the rents of the landed interest or the dividends of the investor and business element, and it is a fair calculation that the governmental bill of costs, direct and indirect, absorbs at least half the income of those masses who depend upon the wage of daily toil. The serf owed his lord three days' labour in seven ; modern governments, and their privileged dependents, require an equivalent amount, but the value of the services rendered in return is barely equal to the labour of one half-day.

Each step in the eternal march of international rivalry increases pressure upon every part of the world's markets, and with it the urgent need of setting a term to the resultant rise in costs. Nations must either succumb and perish, or there must be a general agreement to replace the present system of expansion by one which will reduce the attributions of the State. Government must confine itself to the naturally collective functions of providing external and internal security. These services, the sphere of government proper, connect with those which attach to provincial and local systems. Like the central government, and impelled by identical considerations, local administration continually enlarges its attributes by trespass on the domain of private enterprise, and local budgets add their burdens to that of the State. These administrations do not possess unlimited rights over the goods and persons of the individual, but, with no precise definition of powers, their claims are solely, and never more than partially, restrained by the veto of the central system which maintains them in various degrees of dependence. This veto is not put in motion

The Society of To-morrow

until a central government considers that its rights have been actually infringed, and what may be called "local autonomy" is the latitude enjoyed by local administrations in limiting the freedom, and taxing the property, of the individual. The actual duties thus appertaining to local systems are by no means numerous. They include little more than a small number of naturally collective services, building and maintaining sewers, paving, lighting, scavenging, &c. Police systems are, properly, a part of the central machine. Yet, minor as are these local services, it cannot be doubted that, in common with the great departmental undertakings of the central government, they could be better and more economically performed by the employment of a private, specialised agency.[1]

---

[1] Compare "Les Lois Naturelles de l'Economie Politique," chap. xiv : La Constitution Naturelle des Gouvernements ; la Commune, la Province, l'Etat.

CHAPTER VI

SUBJECTION AND SOVEREIGNTY OF THE INDIVIDUAL

WE have seen that subjection of the weak by the strong is an inseparable consequence of the State of War, since only the stimulus of proprietary right can change the strong man's interest in his weaker competitors from that of a spoiler and destroyer to one of protection. Thanks to many moral and material advances, and a whole series of transitions, the servant, serf, or slave became his own proprietor. But, although freed from the domination of a master, he remained member of a community or nation, and consequently subject to the power erected by this community or nation for its better preservation from the risks of destruction or subjection, which are consequences of a State of War. This power was, for these purposes, invested with an unlimited right of disposition over the lives and goods of

The Society of To-morrow

all members—a subjection effectively negativing the sovereignty of the individual. However seriously he might be declared sovereign master of himself, his goods and life, the individual was still controlled by a power invested with rights which took precedence of his own. Hence, emerging from bondage to become member of a reputedly free nation, he soon began to devise means of defence against abuse on the part of those who controlled this right. Agents, bearing his mandate, proved incapable of restraining that abuse. Then the nations rose against the proprietary oligarchies in the State, seized this right, and entrusted its exercise to officers of their own. But all in vain. Abuses reappeared, and not only in States maintaining the old system of an hereditary chief, who monopolises the sovereign powers of the oligarchy of which he is head. They appeared, also, in those States where the governmental right of unrestricted disposition over the life and property of citizens was entrusted to the direct agents of those citizens. The sole possible remedy—to curtail this subjection with its priority of claims over those of the sovereignty of the individual, is incompatible with a State of War. The abuse must continue with the continuance of that

Subjection and Sovereignty

state, since the power charged with ensuring nations against unlimited risks must itself be invested with a correspondingly unlimited right of disposition over the lives and property of all citizens.

But the situation changes at once when we substitute a State of Peace for the State of War, and sanction the liberty of each State by the collective guarantee of the association. The coercive power of such a guarantee might not suffice to end all wars, but it must reduce risks of aggression within bounds assurable at a nominal premium. Nor could it, any longer, justify that absolute subjection of the sovereignty of the individual, which is inseparable from present conditions. A State of Peace would reduce this subjection to the single obligation of a minimum premium, payable on behalf of the collective assurance of the nations, and continually reducible until abolished by the extension of civilisation.

The sovereignty of the individual will—to conclude—be the basis of the political system of the future community. This sovereignty no longer belongs to the associated owners of a territory and its inhabitants, slave or subject; nor to an idealised entity inheriting from the political establishment of its predecessor, and invested with his unrestricted claims upon the life and property of the individual. It will belong to the individual himself, no more a subject but proper master and sovereign of his person, free to labour, to exchange the products of his labour; to lend, give, devise, do all things as his will directs him. He will dispose, as he pleases, of the forces and materials which minister to his physical, intellectual, and moral needs. But the very nature of certain of these needs—so essential is security to the human race—cannot be satisfied by individual action. Individual consumers of security must therefore associate to produce this service in an efficient and economical manner. Their association will treat, through agents and in market overt, with an undertaker—be it a "firm" or "company"—possessing the capital and knowledge necessary for the production of this service of assurance. Like any other system of insurance, that of individual life, liberty, and property, is subject to two conditions. The first condition is one of price; a premium must be paid, equal in amount to the costs of production plus a profit. The second condition is technical. The party ensured must submit to such obligations as are

Subjection and Sovereignty

indispensable to producing the service assured. These conditions are matter for bargain between agents of the associated consumers and those of the company undertaking risks of the particular class, and a contract, terminable as it may suit the parties to agree, will embody the conditions when arranged.

Similar contracts will supply other naturally collective needs, such as communications, public health, &c. A small association in need of these services will make a direct contract with the undertakers of the service desired; large associations will contract through their elected representatives. In these several cases the individual exercises his sovereignty collectively, whether through representatives or by direct treaty. But he will minister to the majority of his needs by direct personal effort.

The duty of representatives (agents) is to conclude a contract, and the conclusion of that contract exhausts their mandate. They may, notwithstanding, be called upon to oversee the execution of such contracts, or to modify their terms should experience discover faults or lacunæ in their form, or should new facts involve some change in the conditions under which their mandatories live. Associated consumers of

The Society of To-morrow

collective services may, also, find reason to execute a permanent delegation. But supervision of the clauses in a contract may be sufficiently guaranteed by the action of the public press, or other free association specifically formed for that purpose; or the clauses may not stand in need of modification. Official representatives of the consumers would be unnecessary in this case, and the nation can economise by dealing direct.

It appears probable that all naturally collective services will be produced by an association (company) having the usual business organisation and system. A manager will be charged with executing the decisions of the Board of Directors, or of the General Meetings, to which he will render public account for his actions. This will be the economic solution of the problems of establishing and maintaining the services of a State, when the collective guarantee of the nations assures a State of Peace.

CHAPTER VII

IMPOST AND CONTRIBUTION

THE real difference between impost and contribution can only be appreciated by remembering how political States were first constituted. Founded by communities of strong men, these communities were compelled to defend their possession, interested in its aggrandizement, and obliged to supply government with the forces and resources necessary to assure safety, and to effect such expansion as might be possible. The resources were a military force, the material instruments of warfare, and means of subsistence. Every member of the associated body of proprietors contributed to these in proportion to the share of territory and subjects received by him at the partition of the fruits of conquest—an allotment regulated by the value of the recipient's services at that time. This was a "contribution," and involved concurrent obligations, or a reciprocal contract, between the association personified in its government, and each particular contributory—each associate. The association furnished its contributories with security and other services needed by them; they repaid the association by providing it with the means of producing those services, and these means were usually paid in the form of "impost." Every partner in the common domain owed certain personal services in time of war, and was also responsible for a contingent of men and means drawn from the subject population of his lordship. The lords taxed this population at will, and were under no obligation in respect of the products and services thus required. If an owner busied himself with the support of, or care for, his slaves; if he protected or assisted his serfs or subjects, these actions were dictated by the same considerations which induced men to feed, or care for, flocks and herds. But there never was any relation or proportion between the imposts, taken by owners in the form of compulsory labour, or —under a more advanced economic system—in the shape of levies of produce or money, and the services which they rendered in return.

The forces and resources furnishing the

Impost and Contribution

expenses of States were thus drawn, as to one part, from the personal services of those who shared the common domain; as to the other, from levies of labour, produce, or money, extorted from the slaves, serfs, or subjects of those owners. These levies constituted the revenue of the owners, and, as such, were partly devoted to the support of themselves and the government of their particular domain, partly to the payment of their contribution to the general funds of the State.

Time, and political and military competition, gradually emancipated the slaves, serfs, or subjects, of these seigneurial estates. They became owners of themselves, and of such real or personal estate as a greater or less number of them had been able to amass by labour and thrift. Hitherto the lord had levied imposts without incurring any counter obligation or obeying any other restraints than self-interest, the point at which his chattels might be moved to make open resistance, or the absolute nett limit of their productive capacity. This impost should, now, have been replaced by one partly consisting of rent upon such land and other realty as remained the lord's own property, partly of a contribution analogous to that which the members of the proprietary community paid to the government of their State. This latter contribution should have had the like justification of an exchange of mutual services, and should have been similarly adjusted to the share in the total benefits provided by the social power through its representative government enjoyed by each contributor. But instead of this, contribution, failing to replace impost, was absorbed by it. When a hereditary chief, whether king or emperor, concentrated the rights of sovereignty within his own hands, most of the imposts which the lords had hitherto levied upon their subjects passed with them. Taxes upon the sale of real estate, customs and transport dues, the salt monopoly and that of mintage, were transferred in this way. As a compensation for this reduction in their revenues, the head of the State relieved the lords of the obligations and charges embodying their contribution to the maintenance and aggrandizement of the common domain. This was none the less a retrograde movement in that contribution, implying mutual services, disappeared before impost, established by authority of the king as, heretofore, by that of the lord. In certain countries, notably England, subjects had indeed obtained a right of consent, but this change did not occur in France and the other

Impost and Contribution

Continental monarchies. There the peers of a house, whose head had become king, were reduced to the status of subjects, and were, as such, taxable at his will. They were doubtless exempt from certain imposts levied by them on their ancient subjects in the form of direct taxes upon the person; but indirect taxes upon goods fell upon them with the rest of the community.

One of the firstfruits of the French Revolution was, as we know, the abolition of this system. The Declaration of the Rights of Man lays down that "every contribution is established for the general good, and should fall upon all classes in accordance with their several abilities." This clause marks a return to the system of contribution of impost; contribution now falls upon all classes alike. To have made this repudiation effective, the imposts of the old system—imposts entailing no corresponding services—should have been abolished, and replaced by a system of contributions, each attached to a particular service. The chiefs of the Revolution easily achieved the first part of this reform, but were incapable of realising the second. They contented themselves with providing the resources, required by the service of the State and the additional burdens of war, from the confiscated goods of the Church and the nobility, and by issues of paper-money. Early exhaustion of these temporary expedients left them face to face with the problem of a permanent settlement. But while the State of War continued to demand even greater expenditure than under the old order—such expenditure as was, indeed, unlimited, or limited only by the taxable capacity of the nation—it was impossible to enforce a system of contributions paid directly by every individual and each attached to some particular service, the burden and benefits of which should be equally calculable.

If the old imposts were not re-established in their entirety, the new forms did but embody nominal modifications, and were by no means always for the better. Any alleviation of burdens at this period, also, is due not to an actual reduction in taxation, but to the extraordinary advances in the productivity of almost every industry which followed the application of new machinery and new processes. Taxes rose rather than diminished, for the regular increase in the cost of war and a policy of protection now added taxation in the interest of influential classes to the legitimate requirements

Impost and Contribution

of the State. It might even be maintained that taxation was apportioned less and less according to the strict dictates of justice, since the continued growth of military expenditure was followed by a disproportionate rise in those indirect taxes which are unapparent as compared with direct visible imposts. Expenditure also advanced far more rapidly than revenue, and nearly every civilised State was compelled to meet its deficits by borrowing. But loans, generally employed in war or in preparation for war, increase budgets without rendering any service to the productive capacity of nations. Thus the service of the national debt of France absorbs a practical third of the entire revenue, so do public charges increase at the same time that the sources of supply are enfeebled.

Citizens of constitutional States have obtained a right of consent to public expenditure, and to the taxes which furnish it, but the right has proved sterile. Their representatives have never checked the progressive rise in taxation and expenditure which has occurred in every State, those advances—as may be proved beyond any dispute—having been no less, but often much more rapid, in the States which do possess constitutions. And this process must continue

The Society of To-morrow

indefinitely for just so long as governments, charged with guaranteeing national security, maintain their right of unlimited requisition upon the life, liberty, and property of the individual. But set a term to this State of War, assure the security of civilisation by a collective guarantee; let the cost of this insurance to the individual be reduced until it corresponds with the now almost infinitesimal risk; let the premium to be paid against this risk be as easily determined as that in any other class of assurance; and the unlimited right of requisition, based on an unlimited risk, will lose its only justification.

Then, in place of imposts, founded upon this right, enforced on the slave by his master, on the subject by his lord, by the nation upon the individual, and controlled, to-day, by parties having an immediate interest in continually raising the expenses of government—imposts bearing no relation to the services which they are supposed to remunerate, and limited only by the taxable capacity of the taxed; there will arise a system of contributions, each attached to its own naturally collective service. The amount of these contributions will be fixed by contract between the associated con-

Impost and Contribution

sumers and the companies, or firms, producing the service required at a figure which competition will reduce to its lowest point. The impost of to-day devours an ever-increasing proportion of the revenues of the individual; the demands of contribution will be restricted to a minimum, and a minimum which is continually decreasing as each advance in security reduces the costs of production.

CHAPTER VIII

PRODUCTION OF ARTICLES OF NATURALLY INDIVIDUAL CONSUMPTION

UNDER this new order the national association, freely constituted, contracts with a firm or company to ensure its internal and external security; provincial and other local associations continue the analogy, contracting for the performance of naturally collective, though local, services. The particular contributions required under these contracts are levied directly upon all associates living within the localities served, and their payment relieves the contributors of all further obligations or services.

The individual, meanwhile, remains free to produce personally, or to procure by means of exchange, those far more numerous products and services which are the natural subjects for individual consumption. It seems scarcely necessary to insist on the manner in which

Individual Consumption

individual production disappears as each step on the road of progress increases the economies obtainable by the specialisation and division of labour. These principles find their natural expression in determining the practical formation of commercial undertakings, which again multiply concurrently with the growth of markets, compete with each other, and consequently — always supposing that no natural or artificial obstacles intervene—tend to secure progressive economies in the cost of production. When a system of contribution displaces that of imposts, many artificial obstacles, inseparable from the collection of the latter, will disappear. These obstacles exist whether imposts are collected for the purposes of the State, province, community, or even of particular privileged individuals, and are little less noxious than the imposts themselves. (Imposts levied for the benefit of a certain class constitute a protectionist tariff.) Natural obstacles are already passing away before extended security and the multiplication and perfection of every kind of communication.

The most important and most fruitful of all the revolutions which came to pass during the nineteenth century, was the enlargement of markets and consequent extension of competition.

The Society of To-morrow

A continuation of this process, with the accompanying unrestricted application of the competitive principle to its extreme limits of pressure and intensity, must reduce the costs of production to a minimum in every industry which is not fated to disappear. All industry will, then, be established and operated in the strictest attainable conformity with the law of the Economy of Power. It must employ the most perfect machinery and most skilled labour, but it must also adopt the most economical and most suitable organisation which can be devised. Modern industry is hampered at all these points by obstacles retarding, and acting as a drag upon, production, and the costs of all such disabilities are borne by the consumer of the product, or service, produced.

On markets, naturally restricted by the absence or imperfection of the means of communication and the guarantees of security, the multiplication and development of industrial undertakings have been hindered from the earliest times. The forces and resources of a family, often of a single individual, have sufficed to found a business, and even to carry it on. These businesses, or " firms "—as they were named on attaining any real importance—were directed by

Individual Consumption

a proprietor possessed of the necessary capital. In certain cases he borrowed this capital at a fixed rate of interest, or on guaranteeing a certain share in prospective profits. The actual worker or labourer was usually remunerated according to a fixed, assured, and prepaid rate known as "wages." Private enterprises of this kind differed in no way from political associations or houses, in so far as the continuation or failure of both depended upon the more or less perfect conformity of their constitution and conduct to the law of the Economy of Power. Most industrial undertakings have been hitherto established on this basis. Competition has extended markets and improved machinery until this system proves inadequate to the needs of the more advanced industries. It is doomed to disappear, certainly to fill a quite secondary and progressively diminishing place in the mighty organism of Production. Private firms are already vanishing to make room for associations or companies, and we shall shortly see why this new system is destined to replace the former.

This readjustment would have been achieved long since but for the idea which prevailed, rightly or wrongly, that large agglomerations of powers or resources were a menace to the political establishment. "No State within the State" was a maxim of government, and governments continue to intervene in the matter of combinations, although the maxim has fallen into desuetude. In no single State is the constitution and organisation of associations entirely free. Laws of Association, limiting individual freedom in this respect, are universal, and co-operation of this kind is further burdened by protective and fiscal ordinances protecting the private house against the society or company by taxing income in the form of dividends, but exempting income in the shape of profits.

The action of governments in regulating and protecting associations for the purpose of production has hampered the formation of companies possessing greater powers and resources than those of the individual firm.

National and municipal administrations have first hindered the formation of such companies by imposing these onerous conditions, and then, for lack of the same companies, they have themselves undertaken to produce services lying outside their proper sphere. Producer and consumer consequently suffer together. Similar intervention postponed, where it did not prevent, the transformation of the firm into a company, partly by protecting the former, partly by laws and statutes impeding the formation of the latter. We have already remarked the great imperfections in the company system—imperfections often neutralising, if they do not outweigh its undoubted advantages over the firm. Had the formation of either been equally free, competition would have long since perfected the company, and its indubitable economic superiority have become manifest.

But, once cease to obstruct markets by the artificial barriers of the customs—a system nullifying the reduction in the natural barriers of space now affected by improved means of communication ; grant absolute freedom in the formation and organisation of companies ; and the company will become the usual, as one may say that it will be the necessary, form of almost every branch of industrial enterprise. It will be the usual form because of its ability to collect the necessary capital at less cost than is possible to a private firm ; it will be the necessary form because it will solve the problem of balancing production and consumption on a market which has become practically unlimited in area.[1]

[1] See the author's "Les Notions Fondamentales de l'Economie Politique," part ii., chapter iii.—Progress and Organisation of Commercial Undertakings.

CHAPTER IX

EQUILIBRIUM OF PRODUCTION AND CONSUMPTION

Articles of naturally individual consumption can be produced directly—by the same persons who need them, or indirectly—as when an individual produces one article in order to exchange it for another of which he is in need. The law of the Economy of Power is daily tending to make the latter process more and more general. One or more industries specialise in the production of every article of consumption, and as each field of industry is shared by several rivals their products or services compete in the markets. The consumer, needing these products, purchases them with products or services of undertakings in which his own capital or labour co-operates; or he obtains them with a sum of money, an equivalent which is exchangeable for almost every product or service.

Every advance that substitutes indirect for

Production and Consumption

direct production diminishes the sum of the effort and time necessary to produce a given product, and therefore enables mankind to satisfy a greater number of needs in a more complete manner. No sooner has man satisfied the primary needs, common to all animal creation than he begins to minister to those desires which distinguish him from the lower animals. But, although the final basis of civilisation, indirect production sets up a twofold problem upon the solution of which depends the well-being, even the existence, of mankind. Production must balance consumption, and the product must be shared among all those who take part in its production—the producers.

Although direct production also encounters the first part of this problem, it solves it with little difficulty. Man produces because production satisfies many needs—the need of clothing, of food and lodgment, of his moral and intellectual aspirations. These needs compete for satisfaction, and—as in every other kind of competition—the strongest conquer, those which procure the highest degree of pleasure, or obviate the greater pain. Not until these are satisfied does the individual devote his remaining powers and time to the fulfilment of others, chosen in the order of their intensity, the degree and vigour of their several demands. The intelligent and provident, however, refuse to follow blind desire; they calculate, and yield to each such satisfaction as seems fit, regulate consumption, and adapt production to its demands. Such calculations may go astray. Too great obedience to the promptings of the moment, and lack of forethought, may expose a man to future sufferings no less acute than his present joys. It is also easy to miscalculate the amounts of production, or the quantity of products obtainable in exchange for a given expenditure of effort and time. A return which exceeds, or is less than, that expected causes an equivalent error in the relation of the product to the need which it is intended to fill. Overproduction reduces the capacity for satisfaction in proportion to the decreasing intensity of the desire and its final extinction; under-production increases the intensity of desire in proportion to the insufficiency of the product to satisfy it. This diminution, or increase, in the power of satisfaction, or—stated economically—in the utility of the product, is not simply proportionate to the relation between supply and demand. Its effects are progressive, increased supply reducing demand, and conversely. In the one case it determines a restriction of supply, in the other of demand, until an equilibrium is

Production and Consumption

restored between the supply of the product and the demand of the need.

Under the system of direct production each individual knows his own needs, and the quantities which he estimates sufficient for their satisfaction. He, therefore, experiences no difficulty in regulating his production, but such regulation appears impossible when we first examine the system of indirect production. It does, however, operate with marvellous precision, owing to the regulative power of competition when free to act without hindrance from natural or artificial obstructions. No individual, under this system, undertakes the complete satisfaction of all his needs, but devotes himself—alone or conjointly with others—to the production of some article that supplies a particular need. Those who need this article compete for its possession, offering another product in exchange, or else an equivalent amount of that which is exchangeable for most other products—money.

Every producer, therefore, carries his wares to market where he meets those who desire them, and are prepared to give something in exchange—in the usual case, money. Their desire to purchase constitutes the demand for his wares, and, since his object is to obtain the greatest possible sum of money in return for a given quantity of goods, the seller's object is to restrict supply below the level of demand, never quite to satisfy demand. But since the exchange value of products varies according to the relative proportions of supply and demand, the seller now obtains a sum of money which is more than the actual equivalent of his costs of production—a profit, that is to say, on a constantly ascending scale.

But competition steps in at this moment, and reduces profits to the exact point necessary to determine production of the article in question. An industry no sooner begins to yield higher returns than the cost of production plus a profit—and such a profit is generally held to be included in the costs of production—a surplus dividend, as we may say, than competition causes an irresistible influx of capital and labour, production is forced up, and the exchange value of the product, as expressed in terms of price, falls forthwith. It does not fall solely because of the increased quantities on offer, but also on account of the lower power, now possessed by the product, of satisfying the needs which determined its creation. Price cannot, however, fall below the cost of production, unless in a temporary and accidental manner, for, as soon as the product ceases to

Production and Consumption

command this necessary minimum, the productive forces engaged in an industry seek other and more remunerative fields. Here, failing complete re-establishment, they perish, production is curtailed, and prices begin to rise. When, on the contrary, price rises above the costs of production, competition immediately induces the reverse movement. This action of competition constitutes an economic law of gravity, which is continually bringing price back to the central point of the cost of production, and the further price wanders in either direction the more active is this law.

The first result of this action of the competitive principle is that consumers reap the benefit of every improvement in production. Nor is this more than justice, since progress does not result from the efforts of the moment as applied to any one industry, but is developed from generation to generation and throughout the entire field of industry. Next, when indirect production succeeds direct production, competition continues to assert its power as a regulator. The individual producer, working for himself, regulates production according to the measure of his needs; and—if he governs these in place of submitting to their dictation—in proportion to the demand that he considers useful. If he finds that his production exceeds, or is less than, his need, he corrects the discrepancy for the purpose of equalising the sum of his enjoyment, or of the suffering avoided, with the sum of the efforts, or pain, entailed by the act of production. Competition maintains the like useful order in the realm of indirect production, approximating supply and demand to a point of equilibrium which follows the aggregate efforts and suffering entailed by the act of production.

But competition cannot fulfil this duty if hampered by obstacles, natural or artificial, nor yet in an unenlightened society. The economic history of any civilised people clearly shows that the action of competition develops according to the measure of the emancipation of labour, and the removal of such limitations as curtail an open market. At a time when the worker was the property of an association of strong men, interested, as owners, in assuring him that security which he was unable to obtain for himself, his products belonged to the lord or master of his person. But, when the master or lord discovered that it was advantageous to free himself from the obligation of supporting his slaves or serfs by giving them the right to work for themselves and to exchange their several products, always reserving

Production and Consumption

a claim upon some portion of their produce, this concession resulted in the erection of monopolies. Men who were granted the right to produce a certain article and to exchange it, proceeded to claim the absolute control of their specific industry. Corporations were formed within each lordship, primarily to secure the producer against exactions by lords claiming increased royalties on the fruits of their production, or bartering new concessions against a payment of money ; secondarily to defend their monopoly of the markets within a lordship from external competition ; and, finally, to regulate production, and so fix the prices of their products as to secure the highest possible rates of profit. Then custom or law intervened to protect the consumer, and a limit was laid down above which it was not lawful to raise prices, a *maximum price*. We have already shown how custom and law were able to effect this result in those trades and industries the nature of which made it possible to regulate production, but was elsewhere ineffectual.[1]

Industry and, in a certain degree, commerce, have now obtained liberty. Most industries and professions are open to all possessors of the

---

[1] See the author's "The Solution of the Social Question," chap. iii.—The Corporation and the Slave.

necessary aptitudes and resources, without any limitation on the number of those who engage in them. With the exception of restrictions and prohibitions designed to handicap the foreign producer, markets are equally free to all comers. Market prices are regulated by free competition, or—as we should rather say—by competition freed from the trammels once imposed by restriction on the number of competitors, the rules of monopolist corporations, or laws and customs ordaining a maximum price.

This sketch depicts the present position, but many causes conspire to curtail the full power of competition, and to limit that regulative action which is its peculiar sphere. For despite the extended markets opened to most products by better security and improved communications, the barriers of the custom-house still divide the vast world-market. Competition, acting on a field thus parcelled and divided, loses part of its power as a stimulant to progress, while its exactitude and efficiency as an agent regulating production are even more impaired. Thanks to protective tariffs, syndicates, continuing the ancient system of corporations, limit production at will and maintain prices on a higher scale than would be possible

Production and Consumption

under a system of free competition.[1] Nor are these tariffs stable, but their continual and irregular changes create perpetual disturbance. A sudden rise in rates curtails supply by eliminating foreign offers; prices follow, and the protected home-producer reaps inflated returns, until inevitable transfers of labour and capital reinforce (the home) supply, generally in an excessive degree. At other times tariff reductions flood the markets with imported goods, prices fall suddenly, and the lower price forthwith causes a restriction in supply. Competition is continually bringing price back to, or near, the level of the cost of production, but its regulative action is, in this way, as continually hampered.

Nor are these the only obstacles to its success. Man has not succeeded in regulating the productiveness of all industries. Agriculture is affected by every variation in the weather and all sorts of epidemic blights, but perfection of that branch of commerce which is called speculation might doubtless palliate this variability of the harvests. If the surplus of one season were withheld from the markets, there would neither be an immediate glut and consequent collapse of

[1] See Appendix, Note B—Syndicates or "Trusts" and their Restrictive Action on Competition.

prices, nor would the failure of future seasons entail enhanced prices and insufficient supply. But, with imperfect means of storage and preservation, the insufficiency of, and too high rates on, capital—subject as this is to the continual drain of unproductive governmental expenditure—with the great existing antipathy to speculation, the regulative action of competition upon agricultural products is hindered by time, as it is harassed by the custom-house in the case of other industries.

Finally, and over and above these natural and artificial obstacles, we must remember our insufficient knowledge of the world's markets. When markets were limited to the territory of a lordship, a county, or a province, demand was practically stable, easily estimated, and production as readily adjustable. But such knowledge has become increasingly difficult with every enlargement of areas. The need for it no doubt creates and multiplies channels of information; harvest figures and estimates, statements of the visible stocks of corn, cotton, wool, sugar, &c., are flashed from one corner of the world to every other. But even if this system embraced every known article of production, and was perfected to the last conceivable degree, the controllers of production would still be insufficiently instructed

Production and Consumption

as to every local shortage or surplus. That information can only be obtained by absolute knowledge of the average profit in every branch of production, and such information is unobtainable until impersonal organisations monopolise the entire production of the world. The very nature of such institutions would compel them to issue regular statements of the results in every branch of their undertakings.

We have now outlined a whole series of imperfections in the existing systems of production and distribution. Each of these imperfections has its remedy, but until all those remedies have become accomplished fact, the action of competition as a regulative principle must remain uncertain. We shall see that this uncertainty entails disturbances hurtful, as a general rule, to the majority of society, and affecting the production, the distribution, even the consumption, of wealth. But, under a system of untrammelled liberty, these causes of disturbance will gradually cease hindering industry and commerce, production and consumption will achieve a final equilibrium, and the point of that equilibrium will be the average cost of production plus the cost of bringing the product to those who desire to consume it.

CHAPTER X

DISTRIBUTION OF PRODUCTS AND THE SHARE OF CAPITAL IN THE PROCEEDS OF PRODUCTION

We have seen how competition tends to reduce the price of all articles, necessary for human consumption, to a point approximating to the cost of production. With absolute freedom in this regard, the consumer should be able to obtain any given article for a sum equal to the expenditure involved in reconstituting the material, and the productive agencies, employed, and in maintaining them continuously at his service. We must now inquire into the manner in which products are shared between the two essential factors in production—Capital and Labour.

The socialist maintains that capital monopolises a lion's share of these products, but the most cursory review of the conditions of modern industry will demonstrate why capital takes this greater share, and how the incessant progress induced by competition tends to reduce its amount.

Distribution—the Share of Capital

All industrial enterprises depend on a certain combination of the agents of production, land, buildings, tools, machines, raw materials, food reserves; also upon human material, directors and workers. The former of these are generically styled *capital*, the latter *labour*. Capital may be applied to an undertaking in the form of money, in which case the producer uses it to procure the materials that he needs; or it may be applied, directly, in the form of these materials. But, under present industrial conditions, the products of an undertaking are usually received in the form of money, and it is in this shape that they are divided between capital and labour.

Capital is the product of thrift. An economical and provident man does not expend all his income upon the desires of the moment, but reserves and accumulates a portion either to satisfy future needs, educate his children, support his old age, and provide against the innumerable chances and accidents of life; or to increase his income by enabling him to take part in some industrial enterprise. He may keep his capital unemployed and available for future needs, use it to enlarge his own business by increasing his machinery or labour, or invest it in another business for a contingent return. He may also loan it to others

The Society of To-morrow

who need it for no matter what purpose, but undertake to supply him with a fixed return—with interest. A man is persuaded to part with capital in the two last cases, first because he looks for a return sufficient to indemnify himself for the privation that he may suffer should his capital be unavailable in case of one of those eventualities which determined its original accumulation; and, secondly, to recoup the risks of investment plus a margin, however small, sufficient to induce him to part with it rather than hoard it in idleness. Such are the essential conditions of the remuneration of capital. Competition approximates the current rate of returns on capital in direct use towards this figure, whether the saver himself employs his capital in actual undertakings, or uses it indirectly under an arrangement for sharing profits or on loan. When the current rate falls below this scale, or necessary, rate, capital is withdrawn or offered in less quantities, since the compensation is inadequate to the privation, or the risk is insufficiently covered. When the rate-current passes the necessary rate, capital is attracted, or the amounts on offer are increased. These two contrary movements are accelerated according to the degree of variation, until they cause it to disappear.

Distribution—the Share of Capital

The share of capital in the proceeds of industry cannot, for this reason, be diminished until progress has achieved a permanent reduction in the necessary rate by diminishing possible privations and possible risks. A general fall in the rate of interest has been apparent during the last fifty years, and has been attributed to increased production of capital, and a progressive increase in the habit of thrift. But if the supply of capital has increased, demand has not failed to do likewise. The true reason for this fall in the rate of remuneration on capital—*the rate of interest*—is to be found in that progress which has caused a larger proportion of the capital lent or employed on profit-sharing terms, to become readily realisable. This has reduced the inconvenience incurred in parting with its actual possession, and consequently the amount of the requisite compensation. Thanks to the possibility of instantaneously realising personal estate, the privation—very real in less advanced industrial communities—resulting from inability to recover or convert capital in actual employment, has vanished. No doubt the capitalist who has invested money in personal estate runs a certain risk of loss in the case of a forced realisation, but he may also be able to sell at a premium, and this possibility counterbalances the contrary risk. Doubtless, also, capital is by no means all invested in personal estate, but the proportion so placed increases every day, and the result of a state of competition is always to reduce the current rate on services and products to the lowest minimum necessary rate. Between the returns on real and personal estate, there tends to grow up an average return, and every increase in the proportion of money invested in realisable property tends to reduce the rate of this average return. When all capital has become capable of immediate realisation, the considerations determining this average rate will cease to include the idea of compensation for possible inability to realise.

This factor in determining the necessary rate of return on capital is tending to disappear, but that which constitutes the premium on risks is by no means in similar case. It is, indeed, so far from diminishing that one might almost maintain that it has risen during recent years. The risks to which capital is exposed are divisible into two categories—particular and general. Particular risks arise from the more or less speculative element which enters into all industrial undertakings, and the great liability of the prices, which their products command, to be influenced

Distribution—the Share of Capital

by all kinds of considerations. They vary with the nature of each industry, the mining industry, particularly gold-mining, being notoriously speculative. Agricultural profits are, again, affected by every change of weather. But the rates of return on industrial undertakings tend regularly to approximate to the risks of loss, and the returns derivable from any one industry approximate to the average profit in all, provided, only, that all are equally open to capital and labour. Competition, again, is always seeking out the most profitable industries and is, therefore, always tending to reduce the rates of return to a common level.

General risks attach in varying degrees to every industry in the country of their origin, and a species of sympathy even extends their influence beyond it. They are the result of wars, of changes in the assessment and rates of imposts, especially of the customs-tariff, and from whatever cause they spring every new tie cementing the comity of nations, improved means of communication, enlarged markets, extends the area of their influence. Every industry is likewise subject to risks arising from imperfect organisation, or the errors of judgment, or wilful misconduct, of its managers. General and particular risks alike also fall on that part of the capital engaged in production which bears the liabilities and takes its remuneration in the form of profits or dividends. That portion of capital which takes its remuneration in the form of interest, and that labour which is remunerated by wages, are only affected indirectly and when an undertaking is on the point of disaster.

The capital responsible for liabilities—in common language, the business capital—bears the risks of loss, and assures the auxiliary capital and wage-earning labour against these risks. But no assurance is worth more than its assurer, and it may, and does, happen that the undertaking meets with such losses that the business capital not only fails to pay the interest on the borrowed capital, but that even this borrowed capital is wholly or partially lost.

Borrowed capital is, likewise, capable of division under two heads, corresponding to the manner in which it is employed. It is either invested in particular undertakings, being sometimes more or less realisable and sometimes fixed, or it is loaned to governments and absolutely realisable at will. Such loans are assured by the borrower, no less than those borrowed by particular industries. Their material guarantee is such part of the national income as is collected from

Distribution—the Share of Capital

imposts, and this may, in the last resort, be equal to the nett annual production of the national activities—granted always that the people are willing to bear this crushing burden. Its moral guarantee is the rectitude of the governments concerned and their promptitude in meeting engagements. The guarantee of the English National Debt, for example, may be called absolute, and the rate of interest in that country may be said to have fallen to the actual minimum of remuneration, with no allowance for assurance against risks. Other countries pay interest at higher rates, which vary more or less according to this risk-assurance.

If the deprivation, which constitutes the first element in the necessary remuneration of capital, is disappearing, thanks to progressive extension of the degree in which capital is realisable, we have seen that risks, and the premium of assurance against them, are by no means following in the same direction. This premium, which includes the assurer's necessary profit, will finally constitute the sole costs of obtaining the use of capital. The rate will fall as each advance—resulting from competition and imposed by the pressure of that principle—diminishes the general and particular risks of industry. Nor is it purely Utopian to dream of a time when these risks will be so reduced that the cost of obtaining capital will be practically nil, or certainly limited to the minimum rate necessary to induce a man to lend his money rather than retain it unemployed—and such idleness, it must be remembered, involves liability for the cost of storage.

But the cost of production is only an imaginary point round which competition groups the price-current and price-actual of a product or a service. To make the price-current coincide with the costs of production, with, properly speaking, the natural or necessary price, competition must be absolutely free, and capital must be able to move, without fear of either natural or artificial obstacles, to any part of the immense world's market where the demand is greatest and the supply least. Moreover, there must be complete, or the best obtainable, knowledge of the varying needs of this market. Considerable progress has been made in these respects during the last century, and this progress will continue more and more rapidly as production accumulates in the hands of associations with realisable capital. The modern Stock Exchange List informs capitalists of the current values of most realisable securities. Foreign values are still fenced with limitations issuing from the old spirit of monopoly; but such hindrances must disappear,

Distribution—the Share of Capital

or become less effective, as the investing agencies —the *Banks*—multiply, and obtain greater liberty and more power. Nor is the time so far distant when the universal money market will be an open book, and obstacles to the circulation of capital be removed by improved communications, and the cessation of protectionist regulations. An equilibrium will then be established between the supply of, and the demand for, capital, at the minimum rate of returns—a rate little above zero.

CHAPTER XI

DISTRIBUTION OF PRODUCTS AND THE SHARE OF LABOUR IN THE PROCEEDS OF PRODUCTION

LABOUR, like capital, has a necessary rate of remuneration towards which it gravitates under the impulse of competition — the rate-current for service. The first element in this rate is the sum of the cost of producing this agent of production—costs of upbringing, education, &c. These costs must be made good if the labour of successive generations is to be continuously available for the service of production. The cost of maintaining the worker has next to be added, and the rates of both costs vary with the nature of the work to be performed. The second element is the rate of remuneration required to induce the possessor of productive forces to devote those services to the cause of production. But if this inducement is indispensable in the case of

Distribution—the Share of Labour

workers possessing enough resources to be able to exist without labour, it is not so for the majority of mankind which depends upon the product of labour for the bare necessaries of existence. Only those individuals who possess an independent subsistence, or such resources as allow of their awaiting, or choosing, the opportunity or manner of their labour, can command a premium over and above the necessary wage of production.

We now face a problem whose importance has never been sufficiently insisted upon. The same agencies which reduce the necessary payment for capital, increase the necessary payment for labour. This effect of the progressive transformation of industry can be observed in the two grand natural categories, dividing labour as applied to production. These are the labour of those who direct the hierarchy of officials and the many varieties of salaried employés, and the actual labour of the workman. As every extension of markets and improvement in machinery increases the scale of industrial enterprises, the functions of the worker—the man who directs, no less than the actual labourer—demand a greater amount of intellectual and moral ability, and a less equipment of physical faculties or powers.

The conduct of a large undertaking requires

more intelligence and character than a small one; there is greater responsibility on every member of the directing hierarchy, every error and every misconduct entails more considerable penalties or losses. This law applies equally to the mere workman. The consequences of a mistake on the part of an engine-driver or a pointsman may be far more serious to life and property than a similar error by the driver of a coach. The labourer in charge of several mechanical processes in a textile factory uses less physical force than an old-time hand-spinner or weaver, but his mind is subject to a far greater strain. He is continually concentrating his attention upon the action of his machines, and the more rapid their motion the greater the call on his intelligence. Where the workman is less capable of proper attention, the speed of his machine must be reduced, and the cost of production correspondingly advanced. Finally, every lapse on the part of an overseer of machinery entails a loss proportionate to the scale of the operation or the power of the machinery with which he is occupied.[1]

Every improvement in the quality of labour

[1] See the author's "Cours d'Economie Politique," Tenth Lesson—The Place of the Workman.

Distribution—the Share of Labour

entails increased costs of production, and the common argument that *a higher standard of life* has caused the higher wages which prevail to-day is therefore stating an effect as the cause. The rate of remuneration rises in countries where improved machinery of production requires a superior class of labour to that which sufficed under the old order. Hence a gradual rise in the necessary rate of remuneration, and consequently *a higher standard of life* among the labouring classes. The standard of life will continue to rise and will reach its highest point when the machinery used for purposes of production achieves the highest attainable degree of efficiency and economy. Then, also, the gulf which now separates the worker who directs from the worker who merely toils will be lessened and the differences between the two classes of labour will be reduced, even in some degree abolished. For this difference has existed on account of the disparity between the powers of brain required by the director and the purely physical powers of the labourer.

The cost of production, which includes the necessary interest or profit, is merely a theoretical point towards which competition impels the actual and current price of labour, no less than that of all other kinds of merchandise. But the case of

The Society of To-morrow

labour presents a peculiar obstacle to this action of the competitive principle, one that affects no other kind of merchandise, or only in a very minor degree. This is the inequality between the position and resources of the employer and his man, the seller and purchaser of labour. At the time when the worker became owner of his own labour there were few cases in which his command of time and space were not far inferior to that of which the employer disposed. The employer could afford to wait for his labour, but the labourer could not wait for employment. He was also, for lack of information and resources, to mention no more of the obstacles which impeded his movements, compelled to seek his wages in a more restricted market than was commanded by the employer's demand. Moreover, laws forbidding remedial association on the part of the workers augmented and affirmed this inferior position. Thus enabled to increase the hours of work and reduce wages at will, the employer too often paid far less than the necessary rate, and a continuance of the system must have reduced the productive faculties of the worker until their final extinction involved both classes in common ruin. But developments supervened until this disparity in the command of time and space as between the

Distribution—the Share of Labour

two classes tends to disappear and the current and necessary price of labour to coincide.

Labour has gained this better position by association and by establishing a common fund which enables the individual to wait, to gain time—a device of obvious value, even if it has led to abuses. The offer of labour, on account of the inferior command of time which it possessed, has been less extended than the demand for it. Restated in terms, the supply has exceeded demand by the sum of this variation. The formation of campaign-funds reduces this variation, and, if sufficiently ample, these funds may even remove it altogether. The labourer's command of time and space remains inferior, but since this no longer enables the employer to tamper with the proper rates of remuneration wages depend on the actual relation of supply and demand, of the number of workers seeking employment and the number of men that the employers seek to hire. Over-supply inevitably reduces wages and a deficient supply as inevitably raises them; neither process will take place for any other reason than a real rearrangement of the relative proportions of these two factors.

Competition provides the remedy on either side. A glut or failure in supply is remedied in the labour market by the same means which regulate all other markets. Rising wages immediately induce an influx from other quarters, and a fall diverts the surplus into new channels. Both effects proceed by geometrical progression, the labour market differing from others, in this respect, only in the greater need for absolute mobility within it. Under present conditions the capital and produce markets are hampered by such restriction, but the freedom of labour is even less assured since, besides natural obstacles of distance and racial prejudice, it encounters the artificial obstacles of protection and prohibition, inspired by the spirit of monopoly, and finally our ignorance of the real state of the markets.[1] The ordinary action of competition is, however, already working towards the removal of all these disabilities, co-ordinating the command of time and space possessed by either side, and so assuring the final possession by the inferior of his just share in the proceeds of production.

From the point at which we have now arrived in our consideration of the stimulating and regu-

[1] See, in respect of our knowledge of the markets, the author's "Les Bourses du Travail," chapter xviii.—Progrès à Réaliser pour Agrandir et Unifier les Marchés du Travail.

Distribution—the Share of Labour

lative action of competition we may begin to form an idea of the future organisation of society under a State of Peace and Liberty. Peace will be assured by the collective guarantee of civilisation; vast systems of intercommunication, already in process of construction, will girdle the earth with a coat as of chain-mail; restrictions upon the liberty of labour, on association and exchange, will be removed. Production will then be free to organise, subject only to a liability for the charges necessary to assure individual liberty and property, and nothing will stand in the way of the creation and development of organisations ensuring the proper distribution of products and a right partition between the various agents of production. In place of the present limited markets for products, capital and labour, three general markets will be formed :—

> A Universal Market for Products.
> A Universal Market for Capital.
> A Universal Market for Labour.

In these three free markets, subject to no regulative agency but competition, production and consumption, supply and demand, will find their proper equilibrium at the level of that price which constitutes the necessary rate.

The Society of To-morrow

We have seen how improved machinery and industrial processes diminish the necessary rate on products and capital, but increase it on labour. Progress, on the other hand, reduces the proportion of labour to capital engaged in any industry, so that, whatever the rise in the necessary rate on labour, there is an economy in the costs of production. One question, however, still demands solution. Granting that it is possible to exactly adjust the supply of capital and production to the demand of consumption, can labour be similarly controlled? This question restated may read thus—"Is it possible to adjust the production of labourers to the demand of the employer?"

CHAPTER XII

THE PROBLEM OF POPULATION

WE may take it as a truism that population is limited by the means of subsistence. Means of subsistence consist, in the first place, of those employments which furnish—in whatever guise—wages, profits, interests, dividends, appointments, the entire income of the world; secondly, of the annual sum available for the maintenance of those members of society who possess no means, or insufficient means, of subsistence, and who consequently depend more or less on public or private charity.

When population outgrows the means of subsistence derivable from these two sources the surplus is infallibly condemned to perish, and Malthus has shown that Nature is not slow to enforce her sentence. Sexual appetite is, however, so urgent that abstention and restraint are the sole guarantees against this disaster, and it is essential for the multitude, in any society, to individually regulate their exercise of these powers according to the means of subsistence possessed by the community.

Among the older societies, indeed up to very recent times, this necessary regulation was a matter of compulsion—at all events as regards a majority of the people. Communities still in the savage state, or belonging to an inferior type of humanity, secured their end by the barbarous customs of infanticide and the putting to death of those who had become too aged to care for themselves. Next, in more advanced societies, but where the bulk of the people were still in a state of servitude or serfdom, masters carefully regulated the procreation of serfs or slaves, adjusting it to the opportunities for their employment. Corporate and local regulations replaced these systems among the commercial and industrial communities where the middle and lower classes had emerged from servitude or serfdom and obtained the right of more or less complete self-government. In the sovereign oligarchies and so-called free classes which controlled the government of States the fear of losing caste and the supposed shameful nature of marriages "below one's rank" continued in the same direction, nor is it admissible to ignore

The Problem of Population

the effects of prostitution, whether upon them or their inferiors. So effective, indeed, were these direct and subsidiary agencies that the progeny of the upper class was frequently insufficient to fulfil all its functions, and was consequently compelled to reinforce its numbers by admitting members from a lower social stratum or even from outside the borders of the State.

Systematic state-restriction upon population has disappeared from almost all civilised societies. Every man in every class is free to beget children at will, and such checks as exist depend upon the individual. But the classes, lately emancipated or only partially instructed, incapable of restraining their appetites, have multiplied out of all proportion to their means of subsistence. Whether their livelihood be insecure, expanding under the influence of industrial progress, restricted by artificial obstacles, taxation or protection, these communities procreate in blind obedience to the dictates of appetite. Imprudent development of public charities, particularly in England, has still further added to the numbers of the most numerous class. Abnormal enlargement of the ranks of labour results, supply outruns demand, and the worker is at the mercy of the employer. Wages fall and the hours of labour are increased, with the inevitable concomitants of heavy infant mortality and a generally reduced expectation of life among the lowest classes. These results, or, in the characteristic phrase of Malthus, "repressive obstacles," tend to maintain equilibrium between the supply of labour and the means of subsistence. The middle and upper classes have meanwhile pushed restriction to excess, and, prostitution furthering the consequences, they have, in nearly every country, survived only by the continual admission of recruits and the infusion of new blood from lower strata of the population.

Such rough-and-ready agents maintain an approximate equilibrium between population and the means of subsistence, but their action has involved a decline in the quality of the people. The lower classes suffered from excessive hours of labour, inadequate wages, too early employment of children whose pitiful earnings must supplement those of the parents, neglect, improper care of health, vicious abuses of the fiscal system, and—last, but by no means least—alcoholic excess. The decadence of the upper classes is almost solely due to a marriage system, which forms their connections according to fortune and convention rather than physical and intellectual affinity. All

The Problem of Population

classes pay heavy toll to the widespread habit of prostitution with its inevitable adjunct of disease.

But individual characteristics are the chief factor in the power of any society, and physical and moral vigour decide the battle of competition far more certainly than fruitful soil or perfect machinery. When a State of War placed the very existence of the proprietary association in the State in dependence upon the warlike qualities or the individual, institutions and customs were all directed to its preservation. Marriages, menacing purity of blood or the qualities required of a soldier and ruler, were forbidden, and education was solely directed to the fortification and development of those qualities. But a State of Peace, involving incessant competition between the nations possessing or disputing the world's markets, brings other considerations into the forefront. Success no longer depends on the fitness of a single class, but upon the physical and moral qualities of the entire people. Competition under the new order may proceed by less brutal and less violent methods, but societies, lagging in the race, will still become decadent and perish. The removal of each obstacle to the natural and irresistible advance of international progress will therefore entail a correspondingly careful adjustment of means, in order that power may not be lost through excess or lack of population, or through deficiency in its quality. The adjustment of population to the means of subsistence, and the physical and moral perfection of man, will then appear even more important than now; more important to the survival and progress of a nation, indeed, than any increase of its machinery or weapons.

We have already attempted—in our book entitled *Viriculture*—to show how the society of the future will adjust population to subsistence, to the opportunities of employment for labour and capital, and to point out by the use of all available knowledge, how the physical and moral welfare of the race may be best assured. We shall here confine our considerations to a question frequently argued, but argued with an ignorance of economic law which has permitted the most foolish solutions. This question is the future population of our globe.

Population is limited by the means of subsistence, and these means depend more and more upon the number of employments furnished by the immense field of industrial production. These employments supply members of civilised communities with the means of purchasing the material

The Problem of Population

supports of life and no rational attempt to resolve the problem of future population can, therefore, be made without some knowledge of the potential development of productive employments. Industrial progress must, in fact, be the sole basis of such a forecast.

Industrial progress has two opposite effects. It tends to displace physical by mechanical power in every branch of productive industry; in other words, it increases the proportion of the material to that of the personal factor. A given quantity of products or services is produced at the cost of less labour, and the quality of the product is also improved. A thousand railwaymen, engineers, mechanics, stokers, &c., transport with ease more material than a million porters could move; or a thousand spinners and weavers by mechanical process manufacture stuffs which an incomparably larger number of handworkers could not produce in a lifetime. It is even no dream to prophesy that science will one day so perfect our knowledge of agriculture that a hundred thousand men—ploughmen, reapers, sowers, &c.—will harvest a quantity of corn which a million labourers could not so much as sow. Granting, therefore, that the scale of every industry has reached its limits, each improvement in machinery or methods means so much less room for human labour, and so many less opportunities for earning a livelihood; the process must continue until industry has achieved its highest possible development, and the population of the globe will suffer a continual and corresponding restriction.

But the same progress which reduces the labour involved in producing a given product also decreases the value of this product, places it within reach of a larger number of consumers, and therefore increases the demand for it. This increase follows that of the capacity of the consumer, and this, in turn, results from :—

(1) The improved quality of labour and a consequent rise in the rate of its remuneration, therefore an increased capacity for consuming every kind of product.

(2) A fall in the necessary price inducing a corresponding fall in the price-current, which again increases the consuming capacity of all other producers, and this whether their savings on the purchase price of this particular article are devoted to buying a greater quantity of it or to purchasing other articles. Every improvement which increases the productivity of an industry enlarges the output obtainable at the same cost of production, and this increase partly benefits the actual

The Problem of Population

producer, partly the general consumer. The extra return to the producer, and the enlarged capacity of the general consumer, naturally enlarge the scale of production, therefore the number of persons to whom the industry gives employment. Industrial progress, then, diminishes the number of persons employed according to the reduction which it effects in the sum of human power necessary for production, but it also increases the number of persons employed by the measure of the additional capacity for consumption which follows a lower cost of production.[1] We must now compare the relative restriction and expansion of employment, and therefore of population, which are the consequences of this double movement.

We can only conjecture the economy of human power which progress is to hereafter achieve, or what expansion in the number of employments will accompany the greater capacity for consumption resulting from those economies. The economy of labour—even when we include that which is expended in producing labour-saving machinery, has already effected a saving of 90 per cent. in the costs of production of certain industries,

[1] See Appendix, Note C—The Effects of Industrial Progress on Population.

but the capacity for consumption of the immense majority of those engaged in productive occupations is extremely low, so low that it can often barely satisfy the first needs of life, not seldom quite fails to do so. We know, on the other hand, that increased productivity can so reduce prices, and so increase wages, as to multiply consumption ten times. Thus the demand of a middle-class Englishman is ten, even twenty, times as effective as that of an Egyptian fellah or an Indian coolie—can, that is to say, command ten and twenty times the amount of labour. It only remains to grant that the potential consumption of any human being is equivalent to the amount necessary to replace the physical and moral forces consumed in productive efforts, and it is clear that consumption will exert the maximum demand when production has been developed to the highest possible extent.

Whether the increased human powers required by the growing demand of consumption will more than balance the economy of labour achieved by improved industrial methods, time must show. We can only assume that they will balance, and that the future population of our globe will not be more, if it be not less, than at the present time. But we may affirm that the capacity for

The Problem of Population

consumption and the capacity of production will advance in the same measure as man's capacity for progress, and that the race of to-morrow may, humanly speaking, be no less superior to that of to-day than the latter is superior to its prototype of prehistoric ages.

CHAPTER XIII

CONSUMPTION

Our consideration of the natural laws which govern the production and distribution of the materials of life has now led us to the following conclusions :—

Competition first acts in co-operation with the Law of the Economy of Power to promote progress. Every producer is incessantly compelled to increase his powers of production, whether by reducing his expenditure of Power, or—which is the same thing—by creating a greater quantity of products by the same expenditure; failing to respond, he is distanced in the race for existence, starved, and perishes.

Competition next co-operates with the Law of Value to regulate the production and distribution of the materials of life. By means identical with those of the physical Law of Gravitation, it now establishes an equilibrium between supply and

Consumption

demand at the level of price necessary to induce production, and regulates the distribution of products between the agents of production, capital and labour, on terms which ensure their reconstitution and permanent co-operation in the act of production.

Production and distribution are naturally related to consumption. Products are produced and shared with a view to consumption, to their employment, that is, in the reconstruction and multiplication of the material, and the physical and moral forces, which constitute the human species. Between this material and these forces products and services are distributed, and the division can be advantageous or disadvantageous according to the manner in which it either ministers to the conservation and augmentation of vitality, or injures them. It is, therefore, necessary to regulate distribution.

It is to be borne in mind that there are two species of consumption—the collective and the individual. Collective consumption is essentially a matter of obligation; individual consumption depends on the exercise of free will. Collective consumption consumes those governmental services implied by the terms internal and external security, and those local services of sewage,

The Society of To-morrow

highways, lighting, &c., which are the proper sphere of provincial or sectional administration. The collective character of these services renders their consumption obligatory, but governments and local administrations have undertaken further services, which are the proper subjects for voluntary individual consumption, and, whether wholly or in part, the cost of these services is defrayed by obligatory taxes and imposts. Imposts were established under the old order in virtue of the proprietary rights of the master over his slave, the lord over his serf, or the king over his subject; and they were attached to the discretionary power conferred by these rights. The collector fixed their number and amount according to his own wishes; he owed no services in return, and the sole limitation to his power was the possibility of resistance by those who paid. The new system, both in fact and in theory, transformed impost into a payment for services. But the survival of the State of War implies an unlimited risk, justifying the retention by government of an equally unlimited right to tax those who consume the security which it provides, and constitutional and parliamentary organisations, erected as checks upon the exercise of this right, not only fail to so restrain it, but sometimes even

Consumption

favour it. Hence the proportion of individuas income, levied for the benefit of the State no lesl than for that of its *protégés*, is now equal to, if it do not exceed, the authorised exactions under the earlier system.

The Society of To-morrow, under a State of Peace and in an era of assured liberty of government, will be able to reduce this part of obligatory consumption by at least nine-tenths; but, however great the proportion of income available for the free use of the individual, this consumption should certainly be regulated likewise. The old system rigidly regulated the consumption of classes in subjection. The rules established in his personal interest by the master, lord, or chief of the State, were aimed at the conservation and profitable augmentation of his property—slaves, serfs, or subjects—and were enforced by material and spiritual penalties, the latter being enacted by the religious authority associated with the secular State. The majority of these rules were beneficial to the individual, and he continued to observe them after his enfranchisement. It does not, however, require a very careful examination of the way in which the free individual regulates his consumption, especially since the removal of earlier religious restrictions, to perceive that such regulation has deteriorated rather than advanced, and that it is now no less defective than that practised by the collective government. A particular point, more especially observable among that numerical majority which was probably emancipated too soon, is the improvident drain for present expenditure upon what should be reserved in case of future need, and as a fund of assurance against the chances and changes of human existence. Deficient self-control is also answerable for a far too great satisfaction of disorderly or vicious desires.

We need not dwell on the harmful effects which follow this insufficient, and defective, self-government on the part of the consumer. Besides himself, the individual damages the society of which he is a member, and likewise all other societies in relation with his own. The man who, with no thought for the morrow, expends his entire income on the satisfaction of immediate needs or desires, takes no toll of present earnings on account of future loss or accident, particularly the supreme accident of old age; who, yet more, injures his productive faculties by debauchery and drink; vows himself and his dependents to a life of suffering and

Consumption

misery. To increase his income is rather harmful than beneficial, since it merely increases opportunities for indulgence in those vices which degrade and enfeeble his nature.

The injurious effects of bad *self-government* by individuals damage society by diminishing the productive capacity of its members and its industry, and these ill-effects are perpetuated throughout the world in a decline in the general capacity for consumption. The consumer, even of the lowest rank, is, however, attaining to a higher degree of *self-government*, as is shown by the immense recent increase in savings-bank deposits—particularly in England and the United States—and the extraordinary increase in the number of insurances effected by workmen. Nevertheless, even the most advanced industrial communities show far too many members unable to entirely support themselves, and subsisting, in whole or in part, at the expense of those who have successfully resolved this vital problem, in most cases, only with considerable effort.

It has long been needful to help these unfortunates—victims, too often, of incapacity on the part of the collective government, no less than of their own personal deficiencies. Private charity found the task beyond its control as soon as the change from the old order put an end to the obligatory guardianship of the master or owner. Public charity had then to step in. Under various names and in various forms, it established a poor-tax and a public fund of relief. Institutions for the relief of the indigent were established, hospitals and refuges multiplied. Misery was thus relieved, but its prime cause—improvidence—aggravated. However insufficient public and private charity may be, they inevitably discourage providence. Their mere existence is equivalent to a suggestion that the individual need not rely solely on himself for a solution of the problem of existence, but may look to others to make good deficits that are too often the fruit of vice and idleness. Nor is this their only evil effect. Socialism teaches that society is obliged to assist its members; to satisfy the needs for which they are, themselves, unable to provide.

This gospel of the socialists—that society is responsible for the misery and suffering of the individual, has led to the so-called socialistic legislation, which begins with protective enactments and passes on to measures of assurance. Having limited the legal hours of female and child labour in the manufacturing industries, it proceeded to similar regulation of the hours of

Consumption

adult male workers. Government next undertook to insure the labourer against accident, illness, and old age, these burdens being chiefly borne by industrial and allied undertakings. That the State should stand guardian to beings incapable of self-protection, and whose natural guardians, oblivious of duty, merely contend for an opportunity of exploiting their growing powers, is doubtless justifiable, however arbitrary and doubtfully efficacious the system may be proved. But this consideration does not hold equally good for laws of assurance. These laws are inevitably subject to the defect of applying to entire classes, while—whatever the capacity of the individual—he is subject to the law, obliged to suffer its enactments, and robbed of the right of choosing a method more applicable to his particular case. They also circumscribe the development of an industry, compelling it to bear a burden which increases the costs of production. But there is a still greater objection. Socialism pretends that society is compelled to guarantee the life and well-being of the individual, but it ignores the inevitable consequence—that government, having this duty to perform, must be invested with the means—a sovereign power over the life and all possessions of that individual. If government is under an obligation to forthwith reduce social misery, the members of society should invest it with authority to regulate their consumption and reproduction, as the master regulated that of his slaves. The panacea for all evils, the last step on the road of progress, would thus be nothing else than a return to the first and barbarous stage of slavery.

No one can affirm that the Society of the Future will not be afflicted with a certain number of persons incapable of usefully governing their lives, and regulating their consumption, without injury to themselves or others. A guardianship, supplementing the insufficiency of their governing faculties, and aiding the growth of those faculties by an appropriate system of training, might be necessary. But we believe that such a guardianship has already proved by no means incompatible with that age of liberty towards which mankind is moving.[1] Parents have always been the recognised guardians of "minor" children, with the sole proviso that a more or less arbitrary date has been fixed for emancipation on the ground of their "coming of age." But minority is not

---

[1] See the author's "Les Notions Fondamentales," chapter v., part iii.—Self-Government and its Functions of Guardianship.

Consumption

limited to those of tender years, and there is no logical reason for rejecting a right possessed by the parent of a child, and by government over those members of society which are incapable of self-government. No reason justifies a refusal to place men, notoriously incapable of supporting all those obligations which attach to a state of complete liberty, under such control as is fitting for one whose faculties of control are so imperfect. Those who are conscious of such lacunæ in their sense of responsibility know the amount of liberty justified by their state.

The possible organisation of a system of guardianship of individuals lacking the power of self-government, in whatever degree, has been discussed elsewhere.[1] Such a system will conduce to progress, but progress will be still better secured by measures extending the sphere of individual self-government, and enlarging the liberty of consumption to the same extent as production already enjoys.

[1] See the author's "Les Bourses du Travail," Appendix page 188; and "Les Notions Fondamentales," Appendix page 437—Abolition of Negro Slavery.

CHAPTER XIV

THE EXPANSION OF CIVILISATION

The nations of the civilised world began to seek means of expansion during the fifteenth century, and the process has never been more active than at the present time. The white man has subjugated the greater part of the globe. America and Australia are occupied, Africa is in process of partition, and the greater part of Asia is already in a state of dependence. Thanks to the overwhelming power of their armaments and capital, the white races meet with little real opposition, and may style themselves masters of the world.

Yet the white man's methods of conquest and domination differ in few essentials from those of the barbarian who once invaded civilisation. The barbarian massacred and pillaged, and only when pillage ceased to be as remunerative as heretofore, did he turn to a permanent occupation of conquered territories and a regular exploitation

The Expansion of Civilisation

of subject populations. When civilisation became the stronger power it used the same methods upon the barbarian and other backward races. Spain and Portugal led, and their rivals and successors—Holland, England, France—have been content to follow. With the fewest possible exceptions colonial systems, resulting from extra-European conquest and discovery, were devised for the sole purpose of exploiting foreign lands for the exclusive benefit of the political and military oligarchies ruling the homeland, or commercial and industrial corporations to which, in return for a monetary consideration, those oligarchies were content to cede the right of colonial trade, and the monopoly of importing colonial produce. The insatiable cupidity and bloody cruelty of the Spanish *conquistadors* has become a byword of history. Their advent in the West Indies, Mexico, and Peru, was marked by an orgy of massacre and pillage, and nothing but exhaustion of the gold, silver, and other movable treasures of those countries, turned the thoughts of these men towards partitioning the land, and exploiting the mineral and other resources of the country, not excepting the human cattle—their inhabitants. The vast colonial territories of Spain afforded ample scope for a fruitful activity on the part

The Society of To-morrow

of its governing classes, soldiers, civil officials, holders of concessions, who exploited their lands by Indian labour, and later—when the native had perished under the lash—by the labour of imported African slaves. A few industrial and commercial monopolists secured rapid fortune by their control of colonial markets, but the Spanish nation obtained no return for the enormous expense of maintaining its empire. Desirously coveted by the oligarchical governors of other States, these colonies required a costly garrison and navy, and were an incessant cause of war. Those wars necessitated increased taxation, harassed industry at home, multiplied the numbers of the unemployed, and reduced the masses to a state of covetousness and misery. By its temporary enrichment of a few families, and their enrichment was only temporary since general impoverishment of the nation soon overwhelmed them with the rest, the vicious colonial system of Spain was the chief cause of that country's ruin.

Nor, if we regard it from the point of view of general national interests, has the system of conquest and exploitation been of real benefit to any country. The governing oligarchies, aristocrat or bourgeois, in England, France, or Holland, may have benefited from colonial pos-

The Expansion of Civilisation

sessions, but they are a burden on the generality which must pay for endless wars, and suffer the artificially enhanced prices of colonial products protected in the home market. And, after all this, the colonies cast loose from their mother countries. In the Spanish colonies the war of emancipation was initiated by native aspirants to civil and military employ, who sought to displace officials imported from home; the leaders in the English colonies were colonists—landed proprietors, merchants, and artisans—claiming the right of their relatives in the mother country to be subjected to no taxation of which they had not themselves approved. Thus to the expenses already incurred in colonial conquest and defence there was now added the cost of combating these revolts. The War of American Independence, to mention no other, doubled the National Debt of England, and loaded French finance with a burden which was a prime cause of the premature explosion of the French Revolution. A balance sheet of a "Colonial Undertakings" account, between the close of the fifteenth and opening of the nineteenth century, would discover a singular inclination towards the debit side. And if it be asserted that expansion of trade and industry, due to colonisation, has been an active cause of

The Society of To-morrow

progress, the assertion is true, but it remains that the same progress could have been secured at less cost and by far less barbarous methods.

After a period of comparative rest, civilised nations have again begun to seek after expansion; but so far from novel are the means employed that, while conquered nations suffer no less than in former times, those which expand do so at a greatly enhanced cost. Under the old system, governments seeking to conquer or exploit nations outside the civilised pale, were accustomed to entrust part of the task—and often a very large part—to specially organised companies. They still delegate governmental rights to semi-political, semi-mercantile companies, but it is seldom indeed that they delegate the task of conquering and administering actual new colonies. The colonial expansion of to-day pretends to foster industry and commerce generally, but its true purpose is to satisfy the demands of particular, and politically influential, classes whose support is essential to the governments concerned. This class, the active element in the electorate, is greedy of public employment, and salaried officialdom belongs almost entirely to its ranks. These men live on the budget, whether they be civil or military officials, great merchants or

The Expansion of Civilisation

manufacturers, and their agents, in search of markets protected from foreign competition. The enormously increased costs of a modern war between civilised peoples, and the difficulty of procuring new territory by this means, have forced the governing classes to go outside the boundaries of civilisation in search of employment for their surplus officials, and protected markets for their merchants. The benefits thus secured by certain classes are as nothing compared to the costs imposed on the nation at large. Taking the single example of the French colonies, these possessions cost the mother country a sum practically equal to the value of her exports to the same places, so that it is no exaggeration to assert that colonisation is the most costly and least remunerative of all enterprises undertaken by the State.

Although the colonies of England cost her less and yield a greater return, there can be little doubt that the balance on their account is still on the wrong side. Colonial Office estimates may be relatively inconsiderable, but the Navy and Army votes increase every day, and are largely necessitated by the obligation of England to protect her empire, and to be prepared for the numerous quarrels which are inseparable from

The Society of To-morrow

a policy of expansion. The English taxpayer supports a destructive apparatus little short of colossal, and little more than a fraction of which would suffice to protect the United Kingdom proper. Impost plays no small part in meeting the cost of that armament, and it must not be forgotten that impost increases public revenue at the expense of a corresponding diminution in private income plus the cost of collection, while, by increasing the cost of general production, it also renders the producer less able to compete with his foreign rivals. Competition daily becomes more acute in the field of industry no less than between nation and nation, and while colonial expansion augments the burden of naval and military establishments, it also enfeebles British industry, and renders the nation decadent.[1]

Nor will the effects of this policy appear less disastrous when examined from the standpoint of the nations thus subjected to their civilised brethren. In no single case has the conquest and exploitation of territory inhabited by barbarians, or people on a lower plane of civilisation, brought any moral or material benefit to the victims. Destruction seems inseparable from

[1] See Appendix, Note D—Cost and Profit of a Colonial Programme.

The Expansion of Civilisation

conquests of this nature—destruction in the act of conquest, but still more from the vices and sickness introduced by the conqueror; destruction of natural wealth through a greedy and improvident system of exploitation which fells the tree to pluck the fruit of a single season.

But a substitution of a State of Peace for the State of War immediately gives a preponderant influence to that majority of the people which is vowed to productive labour. This class finds little use in expending blood and treasure on an empty pursuit of conquest, only profitable to a minority of civil and military officials and certain privileged merchants. While necessity, consequent on the pressure of universal competition, compels it to decrease its costs of production to a minimum, it is cheaper to delegate the acquisition and exploitation of countries, still without the civilised pale, to free " Colonising Companies," whose action in extending civilisation will be no less rapid, more sure, and much more economical.

The present system by which the government of a State undertakes these functions and the taxpayers support the cost, appropriates all profits to the governing class in the mother country. The interest of the conquered State and its now subject population is wholly subordinated, and invariably sacrificed, to that of the conqueror and master. Substitute the agency of companies, constituted without limitation as to the period of their duration, and with no restrictions on the choice of personnel or method and—the enterprise being at their proper risk and peril—they will take good care that the wealth of countries, hitherto occupied by backward or decadent races, is exploited on the most scientific lines. Such companies will have every interest in developing the productive faculties of their subjects, and will be entirely ready to ameliorate their moral and material condition. Civilisation will thus be extended without recourse to the present barbarous and costly processes of conquest.[1]

[1] See the author's pamphlet, entitled, "La Conquête de la Chine," C. Mucquardt, Brussels, and Williams and Norgate, London, 1856.

CHAPTER XV

SUMMARY AND CONCLUSION

Although man shares many of his faculties with the rest of animal creation, he only possesses others, or enjoys them in a greater degree. This advantage, coupled with an organism peculiarly adapted to the practical application of any faculty, completes the endowment by which he was enabled to rise superior to all rivals, and to achieve civilisation. Man is the subject of our investigations, and it is unnecessary to discuss whether his superiority is due to one final act of creation, or whether it is no more than the product of a lengthy process of evolution, triumphant issue of an Intelligence clothed in material form. For present purposes, we need investigate nothing more than—" What was the environment in which this being was placed, and what is the scope of his activities?"

Man is an organism composed of matter and

vital forces, and failure to nourish these forces entails waste and ultimate destruction. The consequence of this need—the need of sustenance or consumable material—implies the corresponding necessity of production. The environment in which mankind has been placed also contains a destructive principle entailing the need for security, or a means of assuring safety. Proof of this twofold need is to be found in the suffering which follows any loss of vitality.

Man suffers whenever he experiences a sense of these needs, but each satisfaction of their demands is accompanied by a feeling of pleasure. They can be satisfied by two kinds of labour—labour productive of materials which minister to vitality; destructive labour, or such actions as eliminate beings and things which menace it. But labour, of whichever class, involves an investment of vital force, consequently a pain. Man will not, therefore, labour unless his action procures, or assures, an amount of vitality superior to his expenditure, or unless the amount of pleasure derived, or suffering avoided, is greater than the liability incurred. It is this margin of gain, commonly known as "interest," which provides the stimulus of human, no less than of all other, action.

Summary and Conclusion

This hope of a margin of gain is the first part of the stimulus exerted by interest. The man who has become a producer immediately wishes to satisfy his need of sustenance, or security, at the least outlay of labour ; or—stated from the other side—the producer endeavours to secure a constantly increasing return for the same outlay. But even this impulse would not, taken alone, suffice to impel man to perfect his means of production or destruction. Every such advance implies effort, a supplementary outlay of vital force with its accompaniment of pain. Nothing but increased effort or pain will induce a man to agree to this additional outlay, and the complementary stimulus, which is the essential condition of all progress, is found in the competition for mere life. Competition for life, for the means of sustenance, began when the multiplication of humanity outran the means of natural subsistence. In the ensuing struggle with rival species or varieties the physically strong became victors, and survived at the expense of the physically weaker. But physical strength is by no means the sole criterion of ability, and the weak were immediately impelled to make every effort to remedy their physical deficiencies by the invention of new methods, improved arms, or tools. Competition

The Society of To-morrow

became the motive of progress, for the one depended upon the other, and the penalty of remaining stationary, still more of retrogression, was total lack of subsistence, a maximum suffering.

The action of the competitive principle upon the early stages of human existence has been traced in this book. Man, face to face with species of superior strength and endowed with more efficient natural weapons, learned to co-operate and to combine. Natural weapons were supplemented with artificial, weaker individuals destroyed that the stronger might obtain a more plentiful supply of food, and when it was finally discovered that more profit was to be gained by enslaving the weak and systematically exploiting their productive capacities, instead of spoiling and destroying, this discovery opened a new and fruitful era of progress, for it involved the formation of political States.

The struggle for existence was now transferred to a new plane. The proprietary association in these enterprises—the political States—competed with such communities as continued to live by the chase and war ; finally, State opposed State. The proprietary association in each State subsisted on the nett product of its subject populations, and as this was taken, whether wholly or in part, in

Summary and Conclusion

the form of forced labour, imposts, or payments in kind, the master naturally desired to enlarge his possessions in order to increase his income. The stronger State did this at the expense of the weaker, and the era of destructive competition—of the State of War—was thus continued on a new and larger scale, victory inclining as before to the side which disposed of the largest forces, the greatest sum of destructive ability. A State is, however, a complex unit. It needs a government—an organisation suited to the conservation and development of its forces, and able to concentrate and control their action; an army—a body capable of attaining the greatest possible powers of destruction; also a population, sufficiently industrious and economical to furnish the means of supporting, and applying, the destructive apparatus of the army. The scale of these advances increases with every development of the army, and every advance, under whatever head, in the various powers of rival States.

States, which were able to perfect these various elements to the highest pitch, proved conquerors in the State of War, acquired a decisive superiority over the barbarians whose inroads they ceased to fear, and became masters of the world. This result entailed yet another, unimagined by any one of the competitors, and no less than the secure establishment of civilisation. War, here, ceases to be the producer of security and loses all justification; its use vanishes and it becomes harmful.

The fact that war has become useless is not, however, sufficient to secure its cessation. It is useless because it ceases to minister to the general and permanent benefit of the species, but it will not cease until it also becomes unprofitable, till it is so far from procuring benefit to those who practise it, that to go to war is synonymous with embracing a loss.

A consideration of modern wars from this aspect produces two opposite replies. Every State includes a governing class and a governed class. The former is interested in the immediate multiplication of employments open to its members, whether these be harmful or useful to the State, and also desires to remunerate these officials at the best possible rate. But the majority of the nation, the governed class, pays for the officials, and its only desire is to support the least necessary number. A State of War, implying an unlimited power of disposition over the lives and goods of the majority, allows the governing class to increase State employments at will—that is, to increase its

Summary and Conclusion

own sphere of employment. A considerable portion of this sphere is found in the destructive apparatus of the civilised State—an organism which grows with every advance in the power of the rivals. In time of peace the army supports a hierarchy of professional soldiers, whose career is highly esteemed, and is assured if not particularly remunerative. In time of war the soldier obtains an additional remuneration, more glory, and an increased hope of professional advancement, and these advantages more than compensate the risks which he is compelled to undergo. In this way a State of War continues to be profitable both to the governing class as a whole, and to those officials who administer and officer the army. Moreover, every industrial improvement increases this profit, for the enormous late increase in the wealth which nations derive from this source necessitates enlarged armaments, but also permits the imposition of heavier imposts.

But while the State of War has become more and more profitable to the class interested in the public services, it has become more burdensome and more injurious to the infinite majority which only consumes those services. In time of tranquillity it supports the burden of the armed peace, and the abuse, by the governing class, of the unlimited power of taxation necessitated by the State of War, intended to supply the means of national defence, but perverted to the profit of government and its dependents. The case of the governed is even worse in time of war. Whatever the issue of the struggle, and receiving none of the compensation afforded in previous ages, when a war ensured its safety from attack by the barbarian, it supports an immediate increase in the taxes, and a future and semi-permanent increase in the interest on loans, those inseparable accidents of modern war, and also the indirect losses which accompany the disorganisation of trade—injuries whose effects become more far-reaching with every extension in the time and area covered by modern commercial relations.

The human balance sheet under a State of War thus favours the governor at the expense of the governed, nor can the most cursory glance at the budgets of civilisation—especially if directed to their provisions for the service of National Debts—fail to perceive to which quarter, and in how large a degree, that balance inclines. This, in itself, affords no guarantee that the State of War is nearing an end, for the governing class, under present conditions, disposes of a far more formidable power than that immense, but, as we may

Summary and Conclusion

call it, amorphous strength, which is dormant in the masses. They, as no one may deny, have often risen against governments extorting too high a price for their services, or threatening to overwhelm them with intolerable burdens, but the success of such movements seldom results in more than a change of masters, and the new governing class has usually been larger and of inferior quality. The result of these revolutions has been what it always must be—augmented burdens and a recrudescence of the State of War.[1]

Nevertheless, this State of War must come to its inevitable conclusion. It continuously and, one may say, automatically drains the resources of the governed, and, since it is these resources which support the governing class, that class must eventually find itself face to face with the end. The same influences that maintain the State of War, though long since effete, will then close it, and humanity will enter a new and better period of existence, the period of Peace and Liberty. We have already attempted to sketch the political and economic organisation which will follow, built upon understanding of the motive forces and natural laws which govern human action. The

[1] See the author's "l'Evolution Politique et la Révolution," chapter ix.—La Révolution Française.

difference between this organisation and the socialistic programme is singularly essential—it will observe, while theirs denies, these laws.[1]

One question remains before we can conclude—the question of the respective parts played by natural laws and the law of human liberty in effecting this immense achievement. And, finally, we should also inquire the end for which this work has been carried out—a work which has raised mankind, moving him ever further and further from his first state of animalism, his equality with the beasts that perish.

Natural laws have played the higher part, for they have been the determinants of that progress which is summed up in the single word—Civilisation. Stage by stage, they have compelled man to advance under penalty of decadence and destruction. The different communities, together forming the human race, have been driven forward by successive applications of the principle of competition for an existence, to invent and apply forms and methods of government, of destruction and production. The forms and methods succeeded each other in response to new demands, and each was the most perfect devisable by the

[1] See Appendix, Note E—"The Economic and the Socialistic Conception of the Society of the Future."

Summary and Conclusion

age in which it appeared. That they should be the best possible, the most efficient and most powerful—should, that is to say, conform in the highest possible degree to the Law of the Economy of Power, needs no insistence. That it was so does not, however, deny any part to the free action of mankind. Such action is subject to physical and economic laws. Man may or may not build in accordance with the law of gravity, but disobedience to that law involves the early dissolution of his buildings. Similarly, his actions may or may not conform to economic laws, but societies failing to respond to the calls of competition, wasting their forces, individually or collectively, instead of preserving and developing them, must fall into decline, and give place to nations which have lived in obedience to economic demands. These conditions have ruled the past, and they must rule the future, but the evolution of the species has tended to a continual advance in the results of individual action, whether upon the particular society of which the individual is a member or upon humanity as a whole. This was not so in the beginning. The intelligence and will of a directing minority were then everything. They led or gave laws, and a passive multitude followed without thought, and without

The Society of To-morrow

attempting to use its potential power of control. A like system too often prevails at this day. But when the obligations imposed by a State of War have once ceased to exist, when the sphere of collective government has been reduced to its natural limits, and individual action has obtained perfect freedom, the influence of individuals upon the destinies of society and the race will rapidly increase. But this increase will entail fuller knowledge, and far more rigorous observance, of the laws which society breaks to perish.

And now—to what purpose has the mighty edifice of Civilisation been reared? Laws, never made by man, have compelled a continual enlargement of his powers over things natural. Happiness is not that end, for if progress has reduced the suffering and increased the pleasures of the race, no one can maintain that increased pleasure has been the reward of those who have actually achieved advances, nor deny that the present has too often suffered in hope of a future good. Less suffering and more pleasure may be accidents of progress, but they are not its end and purpose. Nor can we define that purpose more clearly than by saying that it is the enlargement of human powers to fit men for a future of which they have no knowledge.

PART III
APPENDIX

NOTE A

THE CZAR AND DISARMAMENT

The Czar's manifesto in favour of international disarmament affords clear proof that kings themselves are feeling the disastrous consequences of the continued State of War. On August 12—new style, August 24—1898, Count Mouravieff, by order of the Emperor, handed a copy of the following Note to the representative of every Power accredited to the Court of St. Petersburg:—

"A universal peace, and a reduction of the present intolerable burdens imposed on all nations by the excessive armaments of to-day, is the ideal towards which every government should strive.

The Society of To-morrow

"The magnanimous and humanitarian views of His Majesty the Emperor, my august master, are entirely devoted to this cause, convinced that such a measure involves the most essential interests and the legitimate aspirations of every Power. The Imperial Government believes the present moment to be very favourable for an international inquiry into the most effective means of assuring the real and durable peace of all nations, and, in particular, for placing limits upon the progressive enlargement of present armaments.

"The past twenty years have seen a particular and general movement towards the ideal of a universal peace. Maintenance of peace has been the first object of international policy. The Great Powers have concluded alliances for this purpose, and the better assurance of permanent peace has initiated hitherto undreamed-of developments in the armed power of nations, which shrink from no sacrifice in order to enlarge their forces.

"None of these efforts have, hitherto, brought the desired solution. The unceasing increase in financial burdens is threatening the very roots of public prosperity. The intellectual and physical potentialities of the peoples, of labour and capital, are for the most part diverted from their natural channels and unproductively consumed. Millions

The Czar and Disarmament

of pounds are spent on engines of warfare which to-day regards as irresistible, but which a single new discovery will to-morrow render valueless. National culture, economic progress, and the production of wealth, are paralysed or miscarry; every advance in the armaments of the Powers ministers less and less to the purpose for which they were created.

"Economic crises, largely due to a system which arms the nations *cap-à-pié*, and to the continual dangers inseparable from such accumulation of warlike material, transform the armed peace of to-day into a burden so overwhelming that the nations support it with daily increasing difficulty. An indefinite prolongation of this system must, therefore, inevitably bring about that cataclysm for whose prevention it was designed, and the mere thought of whose horrors makes every mind shudder. To set a final term on these armaments, and to discover a means of preventing calamities that threaten the entire world, is the supreme duty of every modern State.

"Filled with these feelings, His Majesty deigns to command me to propose a Conference, on the subject of this grave problem, between all governments having representatives accredited to the Imperial Court.

The Society of To-morrow

"This Conference should, by God's help, be of fortunate omen for the opening century. It would weld into one powerful unity the efforts of all those States which sincerely seek the triumph of the grand ideal of universal peace, despite every trouble and discord.

"At the same time it should also cement their efforts by a common consecration to those principles of equity and of right on which the security of States and the well-being of nations repose."

Count Mouravieff likewise addressed the following circular, under date December 30, 1898—January 13, 1899, new style—to the representatives of the Powers at St. Petersburg, summarising the points suggested for consideration at the Conference:—

"When, last August, my august master commanded me to propose to the governments, represented at the Court of St. Petersburg, a Conference to inquire into the most efficacious means of assuring the benefits of a real and durable peace to all nations, and, more especially, of placing a term on the present progressive augmentation of armaments, nothing seemed to be opposed to a more or less early realisation of this project.

The Czar and Disarmament

"The eager response of almost every Power to the suggestion of the Imperial Government could not fail to justify this belief. Very conscious of the sympathetic terms, in which most governments couched their reply, the Imperial Cabinet, at the same time, experienced lively satisfaction from the warm testimonies of sympathy addressed to it from every side, and still continuing to arrive, by every social rank and from every quarter of the world.

"Despite the great current of opinion favouring the idea of a general pacification, the aspect of the political horizon has sensibly changed. Several Powers have lately increased their armaments, vying with one another in the development of their military power, a situation the uncertainty of which might well cause inquiry as to whether the Powers find the present moment opportune for an international discussion of the ideas set forth in the circular of August 12th.

"Continuing to hope that the elements of trouble clouding the political horizon will soon give place to dispositions of a calmer kind, and such as will be favourable to the success of the projected conference, the Imperial Government is of opinion that an immediate exchange of preliminary ideas in this sense can be undertaken between the Powers, and an inquiry initiated without delay into the means of limiting the present augmentation of military and naval armaments—a question evidently becoming more and more urgent in view of recent developments in the line of these armaments—and to prepare a way for the discussion of questions touching the possibility of substituting the pacific action of international diplomacy for the arbitrament of force.

"In the event of the Powers considering the present moment favourable for calling a Conference on this basis, it will certainly be useful to have some understanding between the Cabinets as to the programme to be submitted for discussion. The subjects to be submitted for international discussion at the Conference may be outlined as follows:—

"1. Agreement establishing a fixed term during which any augmentation of armaments, by sea or on land, shall be forbidden, and likewise any increase of the appropriations devoted thereto: a general discussion as to possible future measures whereby these armaments and budgets may hereafter be reduced.

"2. Agreement forbidding the introduction, for army or navy, of new firearms of whatever kind, or of powders of higher power than those

The Czar and Disarmament

already in use, whether for guns or small arms.

" 3. Restrictions on the use, in wars by land, of such high explosives as are already employed, and prohibition on the discharge of projectiles or explosives of any kind from balloons or similar machines.

" 4. Prohibition on the use, in naval wars, of submarine torpedo boats, divers, or any destructive engines of such nature, and an undertaking to construct no new rams.

" 5. Application to naval wars of the stipulations of the Geneva Convention of 1864, on the basis of the additional articles of 1868.

" 6. Neutralisation, under the same head, of vessels or boats rescuing the shipwrecked, whether during or after a naval engagement.

" 7. Revision of the declaration of the uses and customs of war drawn up by the Conference of Brussels in 1874, but unratified to the present date.

" 8. Acceptance in principle of the custom of good offices, mediation, and optional arbitration, in suitable cases, with the intention of avoiding armed conflict between nations ; agreement as to the methods of applying these principles and establishing a uniform system for all such cases.

The Society of To-morrow

"Always understanding that all question of the political relations of States, the present status as established by treaty, and also, in general, all questions not directly included in the programme adopted by the Cabinets, will be entirely excluded from the deliberations of the Conference.

"In addressing to you, Sir, this request that you will take the sense of your government on the subject of this communication, I beg to add that in the interests of the great cause so near to his heart, my august master, His Imperial Majesty, considers that the Conference should not sit in the capital of one of the Great Powers—centres of so many political interests which might prejudice deliberations upon a theme commanding the equal interest of every country."

Following this Note, the *Official Messenger* published a highly statistical article enumerating the military forces of all the Powers.

"The forces of Russia are more considerable than those of any other European country. Her peace establishment, with an annual conscription of 280,000 men, exceeds 1,000,000 men. On a mobilisation, Russia can take the field with 2,500,000 men, excluding a reserve and

The Czar and Disarmament

militia which totals to 6,947,000. Russia, therefore, disposes of nearly 9,000,000 trained soldiers. France stands second with a permanency of 589,000, and a war footing of 2,500,000. Her total, reserves included, is 4,370,000. The German army, whose organisation is especially perfect, has a peace effective of 585,000, and can mobilise 2,230,000 within ten days. Including reserves, Germany can take the field with 4,300,000 trained men of all arms.

"The permanent forces of Austria-Hungary stand at 365,000, rising 2,500,000 on mobilisation, or, including reserves, 4,000,000 combatants. Italy's establishment of 174,000 is transformable into a force of 1,473,000, plus 727,000 reservists—2,200,000 in all. Great Britain stands last on the list with the comparatively small figure of 220,000, or, with the volunteers and militia, a maximum total of 720,000.

"Figures give but a partial idea of the power of the European armies, for it is hard to grasp the real meaning of a million soldiers. It is easy to say that Russia can put 7,000,000 men in the field in time of war, but an enumeration would be difficult, the work of several months. As giving some idea of the accidents of these immense numbers, the French army, extended in line formation, would cover a distance of 520 kilometres (some 325 miles), that of Germany 510 kilometres (318¾ miles), Austria-Hungary 460 kilometres (287½ miles), and Italy 230 kilometres (143¾ miles).

"Europe is, in short, a vast camp, and every European spends a part of his life in barracks. The relative proportion of military to civil population are: in France 11 per cent.; Germany 8½ per cent., or 11 per cent. of the males; Austria-Hungary a trifle over 9 per cent; Italy one-seventh of the male population. The proportion in Russia is 2½ per cent. of the total population.

"The open spaces of Paris cover 7,802 hectares (19,278¾ acres)—exactly one-quarter of the free area of London. The combined forces of the five chief Powers would occupy twice the acreage of London's open spaces, and eight times those of Paris. The combined reservists of these Powers would require room equal to the entire open ground of London, and four times the open spaces of Paris. To review the armies of the five chief Continental Powers it would be necessary to provide a space equal to twenty times the entire superficial area of the City of Paris.

"The permanent forces of Europe number

The Czar and Disarmament

4,250,000 men, on mobilisation 16,410,000, or, with all reserves, 34,000,000. In column of line this colossal army would stretch from Paris to St. Petersburg, and would represent 10 per cent. of the aggregate, or 20 per cent. of the combined male, population of the Continent.

"The armies of Asia—ignoring petty States—total 500,000 on a peace footing. The Chinese army is not capable of any accurate estimate, but is supposed to stand at nearly 1,200,000, many of whom are merely armed with bows and arrows. Japan, on the contrary, is admirably organised and armed. The indigenous forces of Africa do not number more than 250,000.

"Compared with European figures, those of the New World are inconsiderable. Mexico disposes of 120,000; Brazil of 28,000 troops and 20,000 gendarmes. The peace establishment of the United States is 25,000, but can be very largely increased in case of need. The Argentine Republic maintains 120,000, Canada 2,000 English troops, 1,000 Canadians, and 35,000 militiamen.

"The permanent establishment of the world is 5,250,000 always under arms.

"The cost of these enormous forces is as follows:—

The Society of To-morrow

Russia	772,500,000 francs	=	£30,900,000
Germany	675,000,000 ,,	=	£27,000,000
France	650,000,000 ,,	=	£26,000,000
Austria-Hungary ...	332,500,000 ,,	=	£13,300,000
Italy	267,250,000 ,,	=	£10,650,000
Great Britain... ...	450,000,000 ,,	=	£18,000,000
Or a total of ...	3,147,250,000 ,,	=	£125,890,000

"The price per head stands, in order of cost :—

Russia	772.50 francs	=	£30 18s. 9d.
Germany	1,162.50 ,,	=	£46 10s. 0d.
Austria-Hungary	1,175.00 ,,	=	£47 0s. 0d.
Italy	1,535.00 ,,	=	£61 8s. 4d.
France	1,633.00 ,,	=	£65 6s. 8d.
Great Britain...	2,045.00 ,,	=	£81 16s. 8d.

"Every citizen of Russia pays 6 francs = 5s.; of Italy about 9 francs = 7s. 6d.; of Austria-Hungary 10 francs = 8s. 4d.; of Great Britain 12 francs = 10s.; of Germany 13 francs = 10s. 10d.; of France 18.25 francs = 15s. 3d.

"The actual military budget of Denmark is not more than 5,750,000 francs = £230,000, but, even so, is an enormous burden for so small a country. If the nations of Europe are constantly face to face with increased debts, the prime cause of their situation is a continually growing military establishment.

"It is possible to base some idea of the actual potential costs of the next war on the above figures. The last Chino-Japanese war involved an expenditure of 1,250,000,000 francs =

The Czar and Disarmament

£50,000,000. A European war must cost at least Frs. 6,000,000,000 = £240,000,000, with no allowance for incalculable loss in men and material. Germany maintains a permanent war-chest at Spandau of Frs. 450,000,000 = £18,000,000—a sum which would be no more than a drop in the ocean."

The *Official Messenger* closed its article thus:—

"By no possibility could expenditure on this colossal scale be productive. It exhausts the sources of national revenues, increases taxation, paralyses the action of the national finances and commerce, and arrests the general well-being. The best minds of all countries and all ages have sought a means of assuring peace without recourse to constantly increasing armaments—by, that is, principles of right and equity, operating through the channel of arbitration, to finally end this barbarous theory which identifies the course of civilisation with every chance improvement—and they are incessant—in the means and methods of destruction."

The issues of *la Revue Statistique* for September 11 and 18, 1898, give the following tables of the world's war budget—naval and military.

The Society of To-morrow

WAR BUDGETS.

Countries of Europe.	Year.	Total Appropriations.		Cost per Head of Population.		
		Francs.	£	Frs.	s.	d.
Russia	1898	770,159,432	30,806,377	6.07	5	0
Germany	1898	731,478,495	29,259,139	14.00	11	8
France	1898	639,987,987	25,599,519	16.62	13	10
England...	1897	456,750,000	18,270,000	11.47	9	6½
Austria	1897	446,826,031	17,873,041	10.77	8	11½
Italy	1898	236,578,283	9,463,131	7.55	6	3½
Spain	1897	198,225,381	7,929,015	11.00	9	2
Turkey	1897	103,263,031	4,130,521	4.30	3	7
Holland	1897	49,830,561	1,993,222	9.96	8	3½
Sweden & Norway	1897	49,211,678	1,968,467	7.05	5	10½
Belgium...	1897	48,406,375	1,936,255	7.44	6	2
Roumania	1898	44,470,355	1,778,814	8.08	6	8
Portugal...	1898	26,344,440	1,053,777	5.45	4	6½
Bulgaria...	1898	23,307,613	932,304	7.06	5	10½
Switzerland	1897	23,200,849	928,033	7.73	6	5
Greece	1897	16,345,312	653,812	6.72	5	7
Servia	1897	14,115,398	564,615	6.03	5	0
Denmark	1898	13,916,334	556,653	6.32	5	3
Finland	1897	7,997,920	319,916	3.10	2	7
		Frs. 3,900,415,475	£156,016,611			

States outside Europe.	Year.	Total Appropriations.		Cost per Head of Population.		
		Francs.	£	Frs.	s.	d.
British India... ...	1897	404,338,202	16,173,528	2.08	1	8
United States ...	1896	264,735,375	10,589,415	3.71	3	1
Japan	1897	120,584,605	4,823,384	2.80	2	4
China	1897	61,500,000	2,460,000	0.17	0	1½
Brazil	1897	52,374,026	2,094,961	3.08	2	6
Argentine Republic	1897	26,529,664	1,061,186	6.63	5	6
Chili	1897	24,174,191	966,967	0.90	0	9
Egypt	1897	12,457,252	498,290	1.18	0	11
Guatemala	1897	10,480,860	419,234	7.70	6	5
Canada	1897	8,348,640	333,945	1.66	1	4
Cape Colony... ...	1897	4,753,350	190,134	2.64	2	2
Corea	1897	2,497,972	99,918	0.35	0	3½
		Frs. 992,774,137	£39,710,962			

The Czar and Disarmament

NAVAL APPROPRIATIONS.

Countries of Europe.	Year.	Total Appropriations.		Cost per Head of Establishment		
		Francs.	£	Frs.	s.	d.
England	1897	554,250,000	22,170,000	13.92	11	7
France	1898	286,956,946	11,478,277	7.45	6	2½
Germany	1898	182,516,844	7,300,673	3.49	2	11
Russia	1898	178,800,000	7,152,000	1.41	1	2
Italy	1898	101,174,846	4,046,993	3.23	2	8
Spain	1897	94,619,619	3,784,784	5.25	4	4½
Austria-Hungary	1897	42,353,150	1,694,126	1.02	0	10
Holland	1897	32,725,463	1,309,018	6.54	5	5½
Portugal	1897	18,122,989	724,919	3.77	3	1½
Norway & Sweden	1897	15,745,141	629,805	2.25	1	10½
Turkey	1897	12,562,807	502,512	0.52	0	5
Denmark	1898	9,134,254	365,330	4.15	3	5½
Greece	1897	7,000,487	280,019	2.88	2	4½
		Frs. 1,535,961,546	£61,438,456			

States outside Europe.	Year	Total Appropriations.		Cost per Head of Establishment.		
		Francs.	£	Frs.	s.	d.
United States	1896	137,773,665	5,510,946	1.93	1	7
China	1897	42,000,000	1,680,000	.12	Under ⅛ of a penny	
Japan	1897	39,154,020	1,566,160	.91	0	9
Brazil	1897	26,873,358	1,074,934	1.58	1	4
Argentine Republic	1897	18,481,172	739,247	4.62	3	10
Chili	1897	16,150,222	646,009	5.95	4	11½
British India	1897	1,761,175	70,447	.06	Under 1/16 of a penny	
		Frs. 282,193,612	£11,287,743			

NOTE.—The figures for China, as given in these tables, are taken from estimate prepared by the English consul at Shanghai.

The Society of To-morrow

The Czar's Note—(*vide* the author's paper in *Le Journal des Economistes*, September 15, 1898)—a Note that might have been written by a disciple of Cobden, came as a surprise, partaking of the disagreeable, to Europe. The noble ruler who inspired it was certainly lauded, his intentions praised for their undoubted generosity, but he was clearly given to understand that the project was quite Utopian. Yet it would, without doubt, be fair argument to stigmatise as Utopian the idea that Europe can continue to support the overwhelming burden of her incessantly growing armaments, and the no less ruinous imposts which they necessitate. It is credible that the working classes, bearing what is practically the entire onus of this blood tax, while the ruling class does not bear a third at most, will one day rise against the monstrous injustice, and that militaryism is the direct road to socialism. But the eyesight of professional politicians is short, and all things beyond their horizon are naturally chimerical.

Still, and even though the Czar's ideal proved barren of results, his action brought this problem into a publicity so great that it can never again pass into oblivion until, and unless, it cease to exist, being accomplished. And we may, in this respect, recall that the "League of Neutrals"

The Czar and Disarmament

owed its inception to another Russian sovereign, Catherine II.—a league which signally advanced the Law of Nations by establishing the maxim that "the flag covers the cargo." Another predecessor of Nicholas II., Alexander I., laid Europe under an obligation by promoting the "Holy Alliance" which initiated thirty years of peace. Nor is there any reason why this example should not bear further fruit, a similar league being constituted on the broader basis of an alliance between all the Continental States, small and large alike.

NOTE B

SYNDICATES RESTRICTING COMPETITION, OR "TRUSTS"

The New York *Journal of Commerce* recently estimated the capital engaged in "Trusts," at $3,500,000,000, or about 50 per cent. of the entire capital of the United States. The books "Autour du Monde Milliardaire Américain," by MM. Johanez, and "Les Industries Monopolisées—(Trusts)—aux Etats Unis," by M. Paul de Rousiers, agree in identifying the chief cause of the erection and multiplication of these monopolies with the protectionist tariff maintained by the United States.

"A champion of Trusts, Mr. Gunton," writes M. Paul de Rousiers, "argues in his 'Economic and Social Aspects of Trusts' that trusts do not destroy potential competition—that is, the possibility of competition. No one, for example, hinders a man from offering the American public

Syndicate Restricting Competition

better oil than that of the Standard Oil Company and at a lower rate. This is, however, untrue, for the protectionist tariff closes the American markets to outside competition in such a way that potential competition is non-existent. Many refiners, were it not for the tariff, could retail better and cheaper sugar than that of the Sugar Trust. Nor is this the sole result of these tariffs, for, besides closing the market to direct competition, they shut out those goods which could indirectly affect Trust products. The Standard Oil Trust's monopoly would be threatened by the discovery of an illuminant costing less than petroleum, but a product competing with sugar in its own province could be shut out by a new duty. The process can be seen in action in every protectionist country. Provence protects its oil by imposing a duty on earth-nuts, and Normandy protects butter by taxing margarine.

". . . This much is, however, true. Although, dealing in a market protected by duties, the Trusts cannot hold prices at more than a certain premium above that which would maintain were the markets subject to the free action of the law of competition."

M. Paul de Rousiers proposes the following remedies against the Trusts:—

The Society of To-morrow

"Directly the formation of Trusts is not induced by the natural action of economic forces; as soon as they depend on artificial protection, the most effective method of attack is to simply reduce the number and force of these protective accidents to the greatest possible extent. We can attack artificial conditions, but are impotent when opposing natural conditions. It is, therefore, not only more profitable, but likewise more easy, to attack artifice rather than nature.

"America has hitherto pursued the exactly reverse method, blaming economic forces tending to concentrate industry, and joining issue by means of anti-Trust legislation, a series of entirely artificial measures. Thus there is to be no understanding between competing companies, no agreement as to rates between railway companies, &c. The results have been pitiful—a violent restriction of fruitful initiative, and no sort of guarantee to the public against the Trust operations of private undertakings. The American courts have given their opinion that this class of legislation is entirely unserviceable. It does not touch the root of the evil, enlarges, in place of restraining, artificial conditions, and finally regulates and complicates matters whose supreme needs are simplification and the removal of restrictions.

Syndicate Restricting Competition

"Even those Trusts, which demand control as dealing with public services, have been left untouched and undistinguished from others, whence further confusion of public and private interests.

"Trusts, dealing in public services, will completely disappear so soon as American administration contrives to resume a normal control of the interests with whose care it is invested. Those dealing with private industry will—with one or two exceptions—disappear when the same powers learn to refrain from interference with the natural conditions of industry and commerce, especially to cease from all protectionist legislation.

"Then, and only then, will the United States share in the knowledge, long since achieved by England, that competition is no menace to industrial concentration."

NOTE C

EFFECTS OF INDUSTRIAL PROGRESS ON THE SPHERE OF PRODUCTION

In a paper in the *Forum* of April, 1898, Mr. W. T. Harris asks, "Is there really work for all?" To solve this problem he proceeds to quote statistics, showing the changes which have occurred in the different classes of occupation during a twenty years' period in the United States.

TABLE SHOWING THE PROPORTION PER THOUSAND OF POPULATION ENGAGED IN THE OCCUPATIONS STATED, IN THE UNITED STATES.

Occupation.	1870	1880	1890
Agriculture and Fisheries	491·1	460·3	396·5
Liberal Professions	29·3	34·6	41·5
Personal Service	184·8	201·4	191·8
Manufactures	196·2	196·3	223·9
Trades and Commerce	98·3	107·3	146·3

This table shows that about 100 persons per

Effects of Industrial Progress

thousand have forsaken the primitive occupations (Class I.) favouring the remainder in the following proportions: Personal service, 7 per cent.; professions, 12 per cent.; manufactures, 27 per cent.; trades and commerce, 48 per cent. Yet, so much have the methods of culture and the machinery employed been perfected that the national output of agricultural produce continues to more than meet all demands. This discovery leads Mr. Harris to suppose that, granting such an advance in machinery and methods as to render the manual labour—the "drudgery"—of one man per cent. sufficient for all demands in the care and operation of the agents of agricultural produce—clothing, victual, and shelter—the remaining 99 per cent. would still find a higher class of occupation. As a collateral argument, he adduces the statement that in the twenty years 1870–1890 the number of journalists per million of population has advanced from 424 to 963; of photographers from 608 to 880; and of piano-tuners in similar proportion.[1]

---

[1] Rouxel, "A Critical Review of the Chief Recent Economic Publications"—*Journal des Economistes*.

NOTE D

COSTS AND PROFITS OF STATE COLONISATION

The majority of the European States allege industrial and commercial considerations, the need of new markets, to support their conquest and annexation of territory belonging to so-called inferior races. The intention is sufficiently praiseworthy, but involves a question of the cost and profit derived from these undertakings. Now it is an unfortunate fact that Spain was ruined by her colonial aspirations, and few recent programmes of the same kind have improved the financial position or augmented the wealth either of conqueror or conquered. The manufacturer or merchant, who spent ten thousand a year in trade incidentals in order to sell ten thousand pounds' worth of goods, would be justly regarded as wanting in sanity, and his family would rightly place him under restraint, at least remove him

Costs of State Colonisation

from the control of a business. State colonisation is, meanwhile, conducted on this futile basis, as will be evident from a glance at the following figures from an article by M. Paul Louis in the *Indépendance Belge* :—

Figures of the Cost of French Colonies.— 5,000,000 francs in 1820; 7,000,000 in 1830; 20,000,000 in 1850; 21,000,000 in 1860; 26,000,000 in 1870.

The year 1880 marks the eve of great expansion in Asia and Africa, and the budget leaps to 32,000,000, rising to 59,000,000 in 1890. The Soudan, Dahomey, and Madagascar, soon proceed to double it, so that it reaches 86,000,000 in 1892. The relative decline to 89,000,000 in 1896 is fictitious and only apparent, for loans and supplementary estimates of this year raise it to a final 100,000,000, and 102,000,000 in 1897. The estimates for 1898–1899 were respectively 81,000,000 and 86,000,000, but the figures are purely nominal and were largely overspent.

The colonial balance of France in these last years stands thus, and this without taking any account of Algeria :—

>   Costs to the home country more than francs 100,000,000
>   Exports by the home country about   ,,   100,000,000
>   Profit, *nil.*

The Society of To-morrow

This statement ignores the costs of conquest and of the initial settlement!

The same article continues: "The major portion of this task has no doubt been achieved in certain cases, but in many of the more important it is only begun. The simple period of conquest necessitated 284,000,000 for Cochin China; 269,000,000 for Tonkin; the Soudan claimed at least 200,000,000 between 1881 and 1898; Madagascar devoured 150,000,000. Between 1892 and 1898 Dahomey added from 70,000,000 to 75,000,000.

"It is probably understating, rather than magnifying, the figure, if we assert that the Third Republic, by embarking on a series of grand conquests, has cost France at least 1,500,000,000 francs (£60,000,000)."

The cost of Algeria up to the year 1898 was more than 4,000,000,000 francs or £160,000,000, and the annual deficit, which is met by the French taxpayer, varies between 20,000,000 and 30,000,000 francs—an average of £1,000,000. And there is yet another account to be met. The protectionist party subjected the French Colonies to the same tariffs as France, thus closing markets which were becoming highly profitable to other countries, England in particular. Ill-feeling was

Costs of State Colonisation

thus engendered—a feeling embittered by, if it did not occasion, the Fashoda incident, and the cause of inevitable extra expenditure on account of the army and navy. The colonies of France are bought at an entirely exorbitant price, and it is quite maintainable that the slight enlargement of markets which they secure is more than countervailed by the consequent loss in the world's markets. The colonies take a few imports, attract a very few colonists, and afford an immense field for the multiplication of officials. The Reporter of the Colonial Budget in the Senate adduced the following figures, which are not without interest in this regard:—

Annam and Tonquin	1396 officials	447 colonists
Cochin China	1966 ,,	262 ,,
Senegambia	521 ,,	367 ,,
The Ivory Coast	111 ,,	52 ,,
The Congo	254 ,,	20 ,,

Colonisation, conducted on this principle, is simply State-protection of the official at the expense of the remainder of the State.

The apologists of this system acknowledge that colonies are costly both to obtain and to maintain, but they cite the example of England to prove the future greatness and wealth to be acquired by their aid. England, say these men, has acquired

The Society of To-morrow

most of her wealth and power by this means. This is the view of the Greater Britain party, headed by Mr. Chamberlain, in that country, but it is by no means the view of the free traders. The eminent writer Lord Farrer, in an article in the *Contemporary Review*, gives a moderate and conservative estimate of British colonial trade. The foreign trade of England in 1895 was valued at £643,000,000, of which only 25·8 per cent., just a quarter, went to her colonies—£166,000,000. Most of this colonial trade went to colonies, or possessions, such as India, New Zealand, and Australia, which give no sort of tariff preference to England. Indeed it is Canada alone, of all English possessions, which gives such a preference, and that only of late years. It is therefore probable that, were England to lose her empire to-morrow, her colonial trade would suffer little if any diminution. The loss might injure national pride, certainly that of the jingo, but it would reduce the costs of production and so secure an actual profit to English industry.

The actual colonial budget of the British Empire is not large, being little more than half that of France, but her enormous expenditure on the army and navy is largely due to the demands of colonies scattered over every portion of the

Costs of State Colonisation

globe. It is the cost of protecting these colonies which causes an appreciation in British production and handicaps her as a competitor on those world's markets which are ruled by the pure laws of competition. Militaryism, protectionism, bureaucracy, and colonialism, are the order of to-day, but their very excesses are already hastening the inevitable approach of their end.[1]

[1] *Journal des Economistes*—Yearly Summary for 1898.

NOTE E

THE ECONOMIC AND SOCIALIST CONCEPTIONS OF THE SOCIETY OF THE FUTURE

THE political and economic organisation of society has, hitherto, varied according to the mental equipment of the individual, the risks of destruction threatening each society, the comparative development of production—the conditions of existence, in fine. These conditions have been profoundly modified, particularly during the last century, by the progress which has transformed the arts of production and destruction, until a political and economic organisation suitable to the past is no longer adapted to modern needs. This lack of adaptability may be considered as the first cause of modern socialist propaganda, since it has precipitated a crisis whose effects have chiefly fallen on the class which subsists on the product of its daily toil. More, it has produced the systems of

Economist *versus* Socialist

social reorganisation preached by Saint Simon, Fourier, Karl Marx, and a host of *Dii minores*. However numerous, these systems all have one common point—they ignore the operation of those laws of nature, which have determined human progress in the past and will continue to do so until the end. Were these propagandists to confine themselves to theory little harm would result, but they generally endeavour to impose their ideas on society by, first of all, seizing that sovereign power which is the attribute of government. Those who are ardent attempt to do this by purely revolutionary means ; the more moderate or timid by more or less legal methods. But government alone can reform society, and that by breaking down all resistance.

Nowise denying the evils, disorders, and instability, following this crisis in the course of progress, the economist, who seeks to find the remedy, must battle with the false doctrines of the socialist invader. The struggle has benefited either party. It has given the economists an opportunity for a closer examination of the ills which afflict the " most numerous and poorest class "—to quote Saint Simon—with the result that they have been able to attribute them to the proper cause. The socialist, on the other hand,

The Society of To-morrow

having begun by ignoring economics and, indeed, every moral science, has learnt the necessity of studying them. However inadequate the scientific spirit in which these men approached the subject, they have learned to dissociate socialism from some of its most gross errors, and a certain number have even forsaken the primitive idea of their creed—that the State must reconstitute and even absorb society. So far advanced from their first position are the more enlightened socialists, that it does not seem idle to hope that further and more profound study will result in an alliance between the leaders of the movement and the professor of political economy proper.

It was in this hope that, fifty years ago, the present author addressed the following appeal to all sincere socialists :—

"Economist and socialist, we may be adversaries, but our ideal and purpose is one. We seek a society in which there will be no stint in the production of all that is needful, whether to support or to embellish human existence. We seek a society where the distribution of these products between their creators will accord with the dictates of pure justice. We seek—in one word—an ideal that may be stated in two words, *Justice and Plenty!*

Economist *versus* Socialist

"None among you will deny this truth, and, if we say that we seek by different paths, that is the sum of our difference. Your way lies along the obscure and hitherto unexplored defile of the organisation of labour, ours down the broad, well-trodden highway of liberty. Both, we seek to lead a hesitating and halting society, nations looking—but in vain—towards the horizon in hopes of a new column of light to lead them by the way whereon it guided the slaves of Pharaoh to a Land of Promise.

"Now, you proscribe the freedom of labour and curse political economy. Will you continue to do this, or will you rally frankly to our flag, and employ all the precious endowment of your nature—your physical and intellectual powers, to achieve the triumph of our common hope, the cause of liberty? For we can prove that our cause is common. We can prove that all the ills which you ascribe to liberty—or, to use an absolutely equivalent expression, to free competition—do not originate in liberty, but in monopoly and restriction. We can prove that a society truly free—a society relieved from all restriction, all barriers, unique as will be such a society in all the course of history—will be exempt from most of the ills, as we suffer them to-day. We can prove

The Society of To-morrow

that the organisation of such a society will be the most just, the best, and the most favourable to the production and distribution of wealth, that is attainable by mortal man.

"When we prove all this—and we can do so—I cannot think that you will hesitate as to your choice. Certified that you mistake the true origin of the ills which afflict society, and the remedies for those ills—certified that the truth is on our side and far from yours—no petty vanity, partisanship of propaganda or system, will retain you on the shores of error. Your hearts will no doubt be sad. You will bid a regretful adieu to the dreams which have enchanted your minds, dreams on which you were nurtured and in which you went astray. But in the end you will overpass their vain though lovely imaginations, and, surmounting your natural repugnance, you will come to us. And we—by God, we will do likewise, can you lighten our feeble intelligences with but one gleam of that true light which shone on Saint Paul: can you show us that the truth is with socialism, and not with political economy. We uphold our system, but only as we believe it the true and the just. Prove us, then, that our gods are feeble idols of wood and stone, and we burn them; leave, with no reservation, the altars of

Economist *versus* Socialist

our adoration, rejecting the accepted return to the rejected, and worship whence we beforetime went forth.

"One with the other, we stand above the prejudice of party, taking that term at its narrowest. The sphere of our sight is broader, the lift of our wings too great. Truth, justice, the true utility—these be our immortal guides through the obscure circles of mortal knowledge! Humanity—she is our Beatrice! . . ."[1]

This appeal, brimming as it is with the naïve confidence of youth, is shown premature in the event. But if none gave ear to it, stillborn in a time unripe, it may yet find hearers. And socialism, allied to the economist, may yet, in that alliance, surmount the barriers of egoistic and blind self-interests, barriers outworn yet clinging about the neck of a transformation which is essential if the political and economic organisation of society is to adapt itself to the changed conditions of the Societies of To-morrow.

[1] Extracted from "l'Utopie de la Liberté"—A Letter to Socialists. *Journal des Economistes*, June 15, 1848.